MW01286191

McSWEENEY'S 79

© 2025 McSweeney's Quarterly Concern and the contributors, San Francisco, California. ASSISTED BY: Annie Dills, Su Ertekin-Taner, Daniel Gumbiner, Raj Tawney, Lily Ulriksen, and Bryce Woodcock. WEBSITE: Chris Monks. COPY EDITOR: Caitlin Van Dusen. DIRECTOR OF SALES AND COMMUNICATION: Dan Weiss. TECHNOLOGY DIRECTOR: Nikky Southerland. ART DIRECTOR: Sunra Thompson. FOUNDING EDITOR: Dave Eggers. PUBLISHER AND EXECUTIVE DIRECTOR: Amanda Uhle. ASSOCIATE EDITOR: Lucy Huber. EDITOR: Rita Bullwinkel.

INTERIOR ILLUSTRATIONS: Matt Panuska.

COVER ART: Marta Monteiro.

MCSWEENEY'S LITERARY ARTS FUND BOARD OF DIRECTORS: Natasha Boas, Carol Davis, Brian Dice (president), Isabel Duffy-Pinner, Caterina Fake, Hilary Kivitz, Jordan Kurland, Nion McEvoy, Gina Pell, Jed Repko, Vendela Vida.

Printed in China

This project is supported in part by the National Endowment for the Arts. To find out more about how National Endowment for the Arts grants impact individuals and communities, visit www.arts.gov.

DEAR MCSWEENEY'S,

Signs pertain to me.

Signs pertain to me?

This is my first-ever question for the I Ching. I write it on the back of a small red square of paper. With a thin ink pen: the question is timid. For the answer I have a Sharpie. This is the method I've devised, from the materials at hand. Other materials at hand: a red scarf; four silver coins (one to witness, three to throw), shoved into my closet years ago by my father, who said, "from your grandmother," and "valuable," and gave no further explanation; an English translation of a German translation of the I Ching, the one with a foreword by Carl Jung.

On the square of paper there is lots of extra space. *Why do…? How do…? Is it an illusion that…?* are words that might fill it, preceding the question, which, without them, looks like a bewildered little cry for help. I charge each shaking of the coins with the intent of these missing words, the incompleteness of my question. The coins are heavy and hefty and don't really bounce in the hollow of my hands. I shake a little too vigorously. I am worried I have not thought this through, I am worried I am charging forward inelegantly. Still I bend down to add their answers eagerly, too eagerly, while my friend builds the hexagram with Sharpie on the red square of paper, line by line.

Dear McSweeney's, ask me: What signs?

It's the Year of the Snake. Last year I was in China for Lunar New Year. It was the first time I had seen my family in five years; during lockdown,

I'd believed I might never see them again. It was the Year of the Dragon, a big year for obvious reasons, the dragon being obviously powerful, and the Chinese dragon being obviously a very cool creature. It was also the first Lunar New Year in China since the pandemic when people were allowed to gather and celebrate. I had gotten married during the pandemic and was bringing my spouse to meet my family. It was the first time someone from my American life went all the way with me, into the deep creases of the mountains where my first impressions of the world were formed.

The dragon is the only creature in the Chinese zodiac who can't be found on Earth. The dragon is yang, prosperity, ruler of the seas and the skies, arbiter of weather, guardian and gatekeeper of cities, capitals, empires. The snake is the dragon's secret sister. Her tongue is venom, not fire. She can't fly or even walk, she's wanted nowhere but slyly slithers in, she is earthbound but footless, yin embodied, cold-blooded, reptile, terrorizer of deserts—but the mathematics of her movement resembles water.

I am a snake. I was excited for this year. I'd had a very yang year—lots of action, it was fun. In my dragon year I had also seen many snakes. Every time I went on a hike, a snake seemed to cross my path. This hasn't happened before or since. My yang year continued. Perhaps the writer in me felt that action must build toward something: my glorious snake year, surely. I looked forward to it.

Then I learned that the year of your own sign is unlucky. You're at odds with the god of the year, and she wants to humble you. Immediately I felt humbled. I asked for help. DeepSeek, the new Chinese AI, confirmed my unlucky horoscope, and advised that I collaborate with the ox and the rooster. I am married to an ox, phew; I needed to find some roosters. A poet told me, "Stay low." A fellow snake texted me a photo of a dozen newly purchased red boxer briefs, writing, "Red underwear is mandatory." Now I understood why my father, a dragon, had been gifted a pack of red socks last year. He'd given me one pair. I pulled them on.

In San Francisco, where I live, the last day of the dragon year was bright and clear. The first day of the snake year was gloomy and dark. My psyche reflected these conditions.

I was trying to buy red underwear. I was wary and uncertain: All my dragon breakthroughs—was I just supposed to retreat now, wait out this dangerous year?

I sought a tarot reading from a certified witch. Certified by me: When she performed the initial grounding, saying, "Visualize roots growing from you into the earth," roots grew from me into the earth. Sitting on the floor of her second-story office, where she also practices therapy, I felt them, starting from above my hips, reaching through me into the floor, around and down the walls, prying into the side-walks. I felt the concrete crack, then, with an animal shrug-shake, settle back into place. I was held there, in place, my ass on the floor. What was her Chinese zodiac sign? I asked when I could speak. "Rooster." She grinned.

My witch laid out a Celtic cross. When she spoke, each card and its position described my situation exactly. I won't go into details, so you'll just have to trust me. Signs pertain to me. It seems that whenever I look for them, they do.

The cards describing exactly the present and near past had been overwhelmingly positive. Two future-facing cards suggested struggle and reckoning. The final card, signify-ing "outcome," was the Devil.

I had asked the tarot, "How wor-ried should I be?"

"Pretty worried," the tarot answered.

At a friend's house, I pulled from her mystical shelf every book interpreting the Chinese horoscope and tarot. Left standing there alone was the I Ching, the same edition I had at home, purchased excitedly and quickly abandoned; the consul-tation instructions had read to me like a combination of finger-dancing instructions and algebra. "Do you know how to consult this?" I asked my friend. She did not. Sheepishly we admitted to each other that we, two Chinese American writers, had learned about the I Ching from *Motherhood* by Sheila Heti. From that book we'd both gotten the mistaken impression that consulting it was easy.

At home, that book of signs calls out to me. After reading Jung's foreword, I am convinced these signs will clarify everything. Unfortunately the consultation instructions are still quantum physics. In the past this predicament might have paralyzed me with shame: in order to understand the I Ching, I must (1) study Chinese so (2) I can read the original text, (3) probably obtain a graduate degree in East Asian studies, then (4) fly back to China to (5) repair my relationship with the family members knowledgeable in matters of superstition, using my improved Chinese, perhaps also (6) study with a Daoist monk. Therefore: paralysis. My dragon year taught me shamelessness. I ask, What would Sheila do?

The answer comes immediately: YouTube.

YouTube was born in 2005. YouTube is a Rooster.

Therefore I am shaking three silver coins. I am sitting across from another friend, whose thirty-year-dark memories of her father counting yarrow sticks came flooding back when, at a launch event for your magazine, I asked what she knew about the I Ching. I am desperate. I need to know. What does it mean when you've been eyeing the universe, that hottie in the corner too beautiful to approach directly, and when you finally muster up the courage to turn and look, they're staring right back at you? Have they been looking this whole time? Do they have the same look—tempting, penetrating, deadly—for everybody? They have enough love and pain—enough for infinity, surely. So what is this ability to make it feel like you're the only one they see?

One of you winks.

A question flutters the air.

The answer is:

Yours,

MENG JIN
SAN FRANCISCO, CA

DEAR MCSWEENEY'S,

I was early to pick up my daughter from the day care beside Lake Alice, so I decided I would sit in the empty nondenominational church that faces the water. I saw a young man fishing beside one of the signs that someone put there, not on the shore but out in the water (perhaps to intercept swimmers), that says DANGER— ALLIGATORS AND SNAKES PRESENT IN THIS AREA. As I walked by he seemed to be turning away from me in the direction of the water in such a way that I never saw his face. It had just rained, and water was falling from the branches of an overhanging syca- more into the shallows where he had cast his line. There were white egrets or, I don't know, white birds attend- ing to the grass along the walkway, and a taciturn girl in athleisure. Lake Alice, a lake with a person's name, seems untouched, perhaps because of the snakes and alligators, a picture of an older Florida, large birds sunning themselves with their wings out- stretched, undistracted like the young man with his fishing line. Islands surrounded by fallen trees and green, uninviting, life-filled water... There is an asphalt walkway that runs beside it toward the nondenominational church, the Elvish one, or maybe fluted curves painted white are actually a Scandinavian thing; anyway, it is a tall and narrow building, always empty, with a lot of fine woodwork like that, and a lot of windows. From far away the windows look like compound eyes reflecting the clouds, the grass, the shadows of cars passing by—they're tinted, so that from the outside, the reflections turn into shadows and it's difficult to tell whether movement you see comes from inside or outside. I thought I saw something moving inside as I approached but couldn't tell. There is one of those little picturesque bridges, probably unnecessary, that passes over a nice section of stream feeding into Lake Alice, marred by another of those alarming red-and-white signs mid-water. It was a very blue-and-white kind of day, very bright, everything dripping from the recent rain, the clouds reflected in Lake Alice, and seeming to sort of stretch out into it, as if draining somewhere. It seemed clear by the time I reached the building that it was not the reflection of cars but someone inside the abstract space, which I knew to be populated only by a single electric piano, pews, and a sort of minimalist altar before enormous windows facing Lake Alice, underneath a lot of the Elvish-looking woodworking, and one of those uppermost cupolas full of spiderwebs... There was someone there. Two guys holding clarinets. One strode toward me, bowing, as I entered, and I was already waving my hands, speaking about my daughter and day care, "I'm early, I just came to enjoy the church, please carry on, don't let me disturb you." "Magnificent, isn't it," the young man said, gesturing with the glowing black wand of his clarinet, while his companion, an older man dressed identically to him, a pair of nerdy, tidy musicians come together to do something clarinet-related in a resonant space—the older man was playing scales, some sort of jazz melody, and

the peculiar smoothness of notes on that instrument was further smoothing itself out into the resonant chamber of the church, shaped a lot, now that I think of it, like one of those fold-open school-lunch milk boxes from the 1990s. Anyway, the younger man disengaged from me and politely began to act as if I were not there, and I seated myself in a pew slightly too close to them, regretting that I had walked forward as part of my effort to convey geniality, so I just closed my eyes for privacy, mine and theirs. They were discussing clarinets, and at some point I looked around and realized there were actually a ton of clarinets on the pews in front of them, it must have been both of their whole collections. This was just at the point when they had been playing these little phrases back and forth, but mostly the older man, not speaking very much, half-seated, half-standing against the abstract wooden altar, letting the music speak for him, and he must have executed one of those little runs just right (it sounded good to me, but I don't know very much about jazz or clarinets) when the younger man said, "It's yours." *No, I couldn't possibly*, the older man seemed to say by disengaging the clarinet from his mouth and looking down at it like a pantomime of *This?* "It's yours," the younger man repeated, smiling, with a decisive nod signaling the gravity of the gift. The older man continued the conversation by playing another little phrase on the glowing black instrument, which floated upward into the Elvish fluted columns— It's yours. At this point I was crying behind my eyelids. After the gifting had taken place, and the older man signaled his acceptance by playing a particularly cheerful and showy little sequence on his new clarinet, they began talking about Charlie Parker, "Bird," I knew that much to know who they were talking about. But I got lost quickly, trying to follow the conversation, and I was not sure who they were referring to by the time I heard the young man saying, "He went to Paris during World War II... It was in 1939... He didn't really sound like that, and he told me"—so it must not have been Charlie Parker—"that he couldn't listen to that recording. Even though—I know! Everyone identifies him with it. Sorry I'm talking so much..." But he didn't really need to apologize, the old man indicated by nodding and shaking his head at the same time. And I opened my eyes then and looked at the plastic Timex on my wrist that I had stolen from my mother (it's okay, she took one of mine as well) and saw that enough time had passed that I could go pick Flora up. I wanted to be able to remember what they were saying but I've never been all that great at following these kinds of narratives, and their words seemed to be floating away like the clouds over and in Lake Alice, away toward something back behind the marshland, some sort of drain for thoughts and clouds. "It sounds great, guys," I said, standing, and reconnecting us over the imaginary barrier we had erected out of goodwill. "I hope you have a good day."

In faith,

ABRAHAM ADAMS
GAINESVILLE, FL

DEAR MCSWEENEY'S,

Have I told you about Kathleen? My checker at the grocery store? The other day she was worked up because she'd rear-ended someone on the street on the way in to work. She said neither of the cars had any damage, and the guy had said not to worry about it. But then, she told me, at the next stoplight she got out of her car and ran up to his window to see if he was sure. She felt so bad, she begged him to take down her number in case anything seemed off with his car. Can you imagine being so pure-hearted? I could tell Kathleen was really still beating herself up about it. It can be hard to move on from moments like that and I told her as much. I suggested she shake it off and she agreed. Of course, easier said than done. One time a guy gave me the finger when I made a minor traffic error and I was in a bad mood for a whole day.

Kathleen is about sixty-five. She has a magnificent blond bowl cut and I can't tell if it's bleached or if her hair has just grayed in the most beautiful possible way. She's tan and fit. I learned this because she's told me that she bikes halfway and then runs the rest of the way to work on Saturdays from all the way over in Ocean Beach, nine miles away. She lives with her mother, who is dying. It's hard to tell what exactly she means by that though; I think her mother's been dying for the four years I've known Kathleen. Kathleen's sister has just reappeared to have opinions about their mother's health, and I'm 100 percent Team Kathleen on the matter. Her sister has been gone all this time and now she wants to control the situation and make sure she gets her share of their mother's meager inheritance. As Kathleen says, hands flicking her imaginary sister and inheritance away: "Fine, take it."

I know I'm not the only one who loves Kathleen. I see people wave goodbye and call her by name even if they don't use her lane. I try to go to the store only when I know she's working and I'll wait in her line even if it's the longest. It's always worth it.

On Christmas Eve, Kathleen told me that at the end of the holiday shifts she goes home and takes all her clothes off and lies naked on her bed.

In the beginning, all I knew about her was that she'd repeat the same phrase in each transaction—"Well, thanks for coming in today"—at least three times. She's backed off on that and just gives me a life update now. I wonder if everyone knows as much as I do about Kathleen or if I have a friendly face that she opens up to. I have a feeling it's the former, but I don't think that diminishes what we have.

I also really love Bob at the post office. He has a very dry sense of humor and ribs every customer, but he also tells them about upcoming construction in the area and asks them if they're going to the street fair that's happening that weekend. One time I brought in a package with a prepaid label on it that had printed to the size of the full 8½-by-11 piece of paper. He gave it one look and told me he thought he knew of a billboard on Interstate 8 that I could rent if I wanted something bigger. He reminds me of my dad.

I was at a Kohl's with my husband's mom a few years ago and

I heard a mother and her adult daughter arguing about a pair of heels. The mom said, "When that baby comes you're gonna need to be able to run after it. If you want me to buy you those shoes, I want to see you run to Menswear and back." I watched as the pregnant young woman ran across the central aisle, touched the opposite wall of the store, ran back, and said, "You see?" The mother carried the shoes to the checkout saying, "I guarantee these are not what you are going to want on your feet in a month."

For over a decade I've been gathering up these details. I'm irregular about it. I wish I recorded them every day, but the document is sizable now, the length of a short novel. I love to eavesdrop and I love little moments of interaction. They make me feel less alone and also like I'm solidly in the world, participating.

As people have gradually shifted to doing more and more of their shopping online, I've felt like something significant has been slipping away in terms of community. I like the weird intimacy of Kathleen knowing what I buy to feed myself and that she gives me her life update in exchange, unbidden (though she owes me nothing). I like that thing where I'm walking the grocery store at the same pace as someone else, but in opposite directions, and I have to keep acknowledging them when our carts pass in the middle of the aisle. I like worrying that someone thinks I'm following them if we have a similar pattern and speed. There are so many stories bumping up against one another when we're out in the world, instead of shut up in our homes, feeding ourselves the stories we've curated on our screens.

I was walking around a mall in my old college town recently. It's almost empty. There's what appears to be a Gap-themed cell phone store, but it's really just a store that sells burner phones in an old Gap. A man outside the store asked me if he could have two dollars but I don't carry cash anymore.

The other day I watched a woman return a birthday card at Target because, she said, "I remembered I hate glitter."

The day before Thanksgiving, employees at the grocery store kept coming onto the intercom to say, "Gobble, gobble."

I stood behind a man at checkout who had a cart full of ten Hungry-Man frozen meals and a single frozen Frontera taco bowl. In that taco bowl, I saw so much hope.

I know that the history of commerce is the new being replaced by the old: first we made and grew everything ourselves, then we started to specialize and trade at markets, then merchants opened up to sell specific goods, then general stores threatened merchants, then came mail-order catalogs from Sears and Montgomery Ward, then came department stores, then malls endangered Main Street. Big-box stores meant no more small mom-and-pop shops. The internet and Amazon and DoorDash wove their ways into our lives and solidified their place during the pandemic when it didn't feel safe to see one another face-to-face. I know we've always survived and adapted and come through, but that

doesn't mean that there isn't a little something lost even when something is gained.

In the produce section, I watched a lady weigh her carrots on the scale. When she stepped away, I weighed my brussels sprouts, and then she turned around to reweigh her carrots. We laughed. "It's hard to tell how much you have," she said, and I agreed.

Thanks for coming in today,

JAC JEMC
SAN DIEGO, CA

DEAR MCSWEENEY'S,
I've been thinking a lot about containers. Does that sound boring? Hear me out for a minute.

I find a simple, calming beauty in objects designed for what they are meant to hold.

Not just dishwasher-fogged plastic Tupperware. I'm talking about a hatbox, a matchbox, a shoebox, a tea caddy, a guitar case, a toothbrush holder. A tiny pillbox with a week's worth of needful medications. An enormous cargo ship full of colorful, interlocking storage containers, each—in turn—holding *what*?

When I dwell on this long enough, my mind's eye will do this optical-illusion trick, blurring the finer details to focus only on the broad strokes and outlines. It's happening as I write to you now, in fact. It seems like *everything* could be a container. Do you know what I mean?

This letter? A container of sentences.

The sentences? Containers of thought.

You might be wondering what got me started on this topic.

A few things. First of all, I was feeling anxious about my daughter's anxiety. It was no huge surprise that she seemed to have inherited it from me. After all, I'd inherited mine from my own mother.

"Mama!" my daughter, age three, has been calling out. "I'm worried!"

She has impeccable timing. I have finally fallen asleep when she calls. What bizarre, surreal idea has her toddler mind conjured now?

"What are you worried about?" I ask as I kneel at her bedside.

What if a squirrel takes my favorite doll? What about dinosaurs, just generally? What if the Grinch—the one who stole Christmas?—what if he comes to music class?

"That's never going to happen, sweetie."

Occasionally, her worries are more plausible.

What if we run out of tissues? What if my dress gets dirty? What if it rains?

I cannot say that such events are *never* going to happen, even if, in the grand scheme of life, they are categorically nonthreatening.

Very rarely, her worries might resonate with eerie familiarity.

What if we left the garage door open? (Um... did we? Worried too, I check. We did not.)

So I was feeling anxious about my newly anxious three-year-old. But how does this relate to containers? you ask.

That brings me to the second thing that happened, which was that my sister reorganized her bedroom closet.

"There was a sale at the Container Store," she told me on the phone. "That place is incredible!"

Adulthood can be so astoundingly mundane, right? I was thinking this as I browsed the store's website while she was talking. But let me tell you— that place is incredible. If you wanted to, you could contain anything.

Anyway, after that call, I thought about my daughter again. I wondered if maybe she had *not*, actually, inherited my anxiety.

Her worries are not my worries. She isn't worried about the health of her loved ones. Or the greed of billionaires. Or environmental collapse. She doesn't even know *what* a president is, let alone what ours is doing.

What she's inherited from me could be merely the *containers* for anxiety.

Initially, this idea brought me immense relief. When she wakes up worried about something nonsensical? She's just found the wrong object to try to fit inside the containers. It reminds me of when she was younger and would delight in placing toy food from her play kitchen inside everyone's shoes. A hot dog in a snow boot. A red pepper in a tennis shoe.

"These don't go here," I could tell her, amused. "Please put all your stray thoughts back where they belong."

Something else to know. Maybe this is less relevant, but it feels worth mentioning: my spatial intelligence is below average.

When I'm putting away leftovers, I have no idea what container to pick. It's pure guesswork, and I choose wrong often. There's a lot of spillover, a lot of wasted space. Or when I try to parallel park? How many strangers have watched and laughed or felt moved enough by the struggle to try to help?

"Is this spot big enough?" I ask, baffled. "Is this container too small?"

That's part of why I keep thinking about them—containers. I don't know what anything really has the capacity to hold.

One day, my daughter is bound to stumble upon the more right-sized worries for the containers she's inherited. It won't be "what if"s at that point; her questions will become "what happens *when*."

What happens when the oceans boil? What happens when you die?

What happens when my daughter wakes up and asks me these questions? This idea made me worry all over again.

One last thing. I haven't thought about this for a long while. But when I was five or six, I went through a phase when I'd wake up my mother in the middle of the night.

"What if I don't love you?" I'd ask, worried.

Can you believe it? I really did this. I woke my dear mother up in the middle of the night—my wonderful and kind mother—to essentially slap her in the face with that question.

I loved my mother. Of course I did. I do! I was just worried because I always said "I love you" but I had no idea, at that age, what "love" even meant. Did I love her? I didn't know. But I said it. And back then, lying, I believed, was the worst thing you could do.

I remember my mom testing out different ways of responding.

I remember her laughing it off. I remember her telling me to stop thinking about it; to "change the channel" on my mind. I remember her losing patience at one point and saying that I didn't have to know if I loved her; *she* knew that I loved her. That this was enough.

Eventually, I stopped waking her up with this terrible question. Why? I think I just saw that lying is not the worst thing a person can do. Far from it. There are worse things, way worse things. The containers for my worry started to hold all of them, those bigger, worse things.

And how did my mother feel about *that*, I'd like to know.

I guess I'm going to have to get used to it. One day, my daughter will learn—as I learned—that it's not the Grinch. Not thieving squirrels. And not the garage door.

For now, when I'm awake in bed with my anxiety, which now contains—among so many other things—the future of my daughter's anxiety, I just keep picturing containers in an effort to calm myself. The simple beauty of an egg carton, an umbrella stand, a spice rack.

Once, my own body was a container for my daughter's body.

Once, my mother's body, a container for mine.

And before sleep comes, and before my daughter inevitably wakes me up again, my mind's eye blurs and I see containers everywhere.

The world? A container of grief. But the world? A container of joy too.

And when that doesn't work, I just browse the Container Store's website and fantasize about how I could reorganize every closet in my house.

Yours, with uncontained gratitude,
REBEKAH BERGMAN
PROVIDENCE, RI

DEAR MCSWEENEY'S,
Today, my sister, who lives in a house directly across the street, delivered the blow that Kevin, my favorite mailman—the mailman on whom I've formed a sort of crush over the last half decade—is leaving.

"Retiring?" I asked.

"Leaving," she told me. "Heading to Philly."

"What's in Philly?"

"He's a stand-up comedian," she told me.

"*My* Kevin?" I asked. "*My* Kevin is a stand-up comedian?"

Until last year, "stand-up comedian" was my go-to answer for the inevitable "if you could do anything" question. My answer now—if anyone asks, which they haven't since it's changed—would be "an editorial member of the *New York Times* food staff." It devastates me that Kevin is leaving and that he told my sister first, but I feel newly and irrationally close to him now that he's a stand-up comedian.

My sister said, "Apparently the comedy scene here is crap."

Well, yes. We live in Kentucky. Is anyone funny in Kentucky?

It's ninety out with only marginal air quality, but I've spent the better part of the afternoon sweating on my front porch, waiting for Kevin. I have so many questions. When I first came outside, I nearly stepped on a recently hatched cicada. It was just past the front door. Its sepia exoskeleton was next to it. The cicada itself—still in the pistachio-green teneral stage—was on its side, its little legs scratching at the air, trying to find purchase. A diabolical army of tiny brown ants was eating it alive.

I know from my stepdaughter, who's fourteen, that my thought, in moments such as these, should be *It's just nature.* But in that moment, my thoughts turned sorrowfully rageful, and I grabbed two leaves, also on the porch, shooed away the ants, and scooped up the cicada. I placed it right side up in a flowerpot under the shade of a hibiscus plant. To the ants, I said, "Little assholes." Where they'd been dining on the cicada, there was a quarter-sized oil slick, black and smeared.

Several hours from now, toward dusk and coming home from a walk, I will notice the oil stain, remember the dying cicada, and check on its remains. My boyfriend, a man in his fifties called Bruce, bald and sensible, will be watching me as I do this. Without being asked, I will explain. As I explain, I will discover the cicada precisely where I left it and gasp. As it died, its body continued to develop, hardening and expanding and turning a darker green. I'll cover my mouth in indignance when I see this and try unsuccessfully to hold back tears.

What I love about the lavender just beyond my porch is the way the bumblebees land on the calyx with a thud, causing the stalks to bounce dramatically, dipping sometimes nearly to the ground, like a football player at the very edge of a diving board. This is something I have seen: many football players launching themselves in quick succession off two parallel diving boards. It was like witnessing a conquest. It felt almost primitive, insane. Some of the largest men bounced so hard and went so high that I gasped in fear.

When the mailman does come she is a woman. She's delivered to us before, but this isn't her regular route. Her name is Liz. She is unsmiling and uncommunicative. She wears her can of dog mace aggressively. I ask her about Kevin. "He's off this week or something?"

She says, "Kevin?"

I say, "Is he off? On vacation? Or...?"

She says, "Skinny white guy?"

I say, "Tall Black man."

She says, "Only Kevin I know is a small white guy."

I say, "That's not Kevin."

She says, "That's not *your* Kevin."

I stare at her mutely.

She says, "Can I hand you this or do you want me to stick it in the slot?" What joke would Bruce make if he were here, after she'd gone? I have a few ideas.

I take the mail, and she leaves without saying goodbye. I've annoyed her.

Later, in bed, Bruce says, "If the situation were reversed, what then?"

"The situation?"

He says, "If a thousand cicadas were devouring a lone ant, would you have tried to save the ant?"

I'm quiet for a long time. The tree frogs tonight are riotous. They groan and hum, groan and hum. After a little while I say, "You're telling me size matters?" I'm trying to be funny. We are both, I think, trying to be funny. But now I am sad, and I start to cry.

Bruce reaches for my hand.

"Did you know," I ask, "that it's been more than a year since anyone asked what I would be if I could be anything?"

He gives my hand a single squeeze, then lets go. He is anxious that we not go down too sad a path at this time of night.

"Is this about Kevin?"

"This is about me."

He says, treading lightly, "Isn't that one of those, I don't know, one of those questions you only ask a person once? What I mean is, does the answer to such a question ever change?"

I sit up in bed and say in my non-bedroom voice, "Of course!"

He quiets me, says his daughter's name.

"Of course it can change," I whisper, staring up at the fan.

"Has yours?"

"Yes."

"Want me to ask?"

"Not if you don't mean it."

"Tell me," he says. "What would you be if you could be anything?"

I watch the fan and think of Kevin onstage, under the hot glare of the spotlights. I watch the fan and think of a perfectly rendered cognac sauce. I watch the fan and think of the grad student I'd not heard from in fifteen years who emailed this morning, just before I walked across the street to my sister's. She was emailing to ask for money, for five thousand dollars, in fact, so she could close on a house that costs less than a hundred grand. The student's father is sick; her in-laws are in trouble; her girlfriend is malnourished—all of them barely making ends meet. "I don't know what your own financial situation is," she'd written. I'd blushed just seeing the words. Fifteen years ago, we were the same age. I read the email twice. After blushing, I blanched. Then I closed the computer and walked across the street, telling myself, Too many details, too much sadness. Too many details and too much sadness to be true.

Now, the fan turning above me, I close my eyes, and I swear I can smell lavender. The football players are bouncing, and the diving boards smack the water with the weight of the men. It's just nature, I tell myself. It's just nature.

"Beekeeper," I say at last.

Yrs,

HANNAH PITTARD
LEXINGTON, KY

DEAR McSWEENEY'S,

I'm so glad we've never met. Don't get me wrong. I would have loved to, but you know how it feels when your life is crazy and you want to talk about the troubles in your heart? You can't really do it with anyone except a perfect stranger. Thank you for being that stranger to me.

I'm on a plane from Italy back to San Francisco. I left San Francisco for Italy months ago because of an emergency: the sudden death of my brother. I was on the couch watching *The Leftovers* with my dog, Quo's, head on my legs, and my father called. My partner was already in bed. I'll spare you what happened that night and in the weeks after, but I'm sure you'll understand if I tell you that before that moment I'd thought I would go through my parents' elderly years with my brother beside me. This will no longer happen. Someone had different plans.

After the death of my brother, I had planned to spend several months living near my family in Italy—I am from there—and instead here I am, now, on a plane from Italy back to San Francisco. Once again because of an emergency. Quo is in a bad way. I adopted him five years ago from a kennel outside of Naples. It was during the hard part of the pandemic and he made it to Milan on the Fourth of July, traveling in a van with a bunch of adorable, tiny kittens. He was nine years old, messy, huge, skinny, and terrified of everything: his bowl, his bed, staircases, trams. Terrified of life itself.

I pushed him a little and even washed him the day after he arrived— he was so stinky and dirty—and soon he started trusting me.

When the summer heat became unbearable, he and I went to my brother's house in the hills of Liguria. One day when I was busy, writing an email, Quo started following some deer and disappeared into the woods. When I realized he was gone, I started calling his name, and running around in a panic. "A dog always finds his way back home," random people told me. How were they supposed to know that he was just learning what home meant?

I found Quo the morning after. He was next to a mountain of bread some hunters had put in the woods to attract deer. After a dark night among the wild boars, wolves, and Maremmano-Abruzzese sheepdogs, with his belly full of bread loaves and one still in his mouth, he was petrified. He looked at me like I was his savior. From that day on, he always fell asleep with his head on my legs.

By the time my partner made it to Italy that pandemic summer— remember when we could not fly?—Quo was groomed and in good shape. He quickly started trusting and loving my partner too. Quo followed us everywhere: a boat in Venice, a train to Rome, hikes in the Dolomites; Umbria; and Tuscany. I even made Quo come on a cross-country drive from Miami to San Francisco. Imagine his happiness when he smelled the wild creatures of Mississippi! Imagine his struggle not to run off into an American wilderness adventure after his Italian one!

Americans started loving Quo, too, for his good looks and kind manners. "He's so handsome! He's such a gentle-man!" everyone said. In San Francisco, Quo and I settled in with my partner and for perhaps the first time Quo understood what home was. He fiercely defended our front door. He barked at strangers who approached us.

When I left Quo to fly to Italy after the death of my brother, his rear legs were not doing well. It was too difficult for him to keep on traveling. When my partner joined me in Italy his cousin offered to stay in our San Francisco home with Quo. The cousin and Quo immedi-ately fell in love. The cousin took good care of Quo and gave Quo his medicine. All was well, until I received word that things were, suddenly, very bad.

When I arrived in San Francisco, I heard Quo barking at me while I was on the doorstep, but he stopped when he recognized me putting the key in the lock. He looked at me with the same eyes he had the morning I found him in the woods, next to a mountain of bread. This time he was also pet-rified, but not because he was caught by surprise. He was clearly in pain. I thought I would have a few nights on the couch watching TV with his head on my legs. I thought I could give him all the tasty treats and loaves that he wanted. No, this would not happen. If you want to make God laugh, tell him your plans.

Why do dogs have to die, dear McSweeney's? Why do brothers have to die? Why does life make us go through this and still we, who are left behind, love it because of the silly and magical and troubled moments we have had with the people and animals we love? How can our hearts still laugh, think-ing of all the pain we have endured?

Thank you for being such a good listener, McSweeney's. Thank you for allowing me to talk things out like I could never do with a fellow human being. It's time for me to get back to my parents in Italy, but thank you for welcoming some of my uncertainties, simplicities, and, most of all, some of my grief.

We've never met, but you're a good friend now. Because you are a fictional character, you are immortal, and for this I am grateful. I don't need any more of my beloveds up and dying on me.

Yours,

ENRICO ROTELLI
VENICE, ITALY

LITTLE WORLD

by JOSEPHINE ROWE

OF COURSE SHE HAS a name, one she was given at birth. And then lived within, almost long enough to get used to it. But that much, the name at least, she is keeping for herself. There are people, still alive, still referring to her by this name. And she is not, has never been, a saint. That hardly needs saying. She is a kid in a box tens of thousands of miles from where she died, with no way back to that place. A kid in a box whose body—*Gott fuck them*—is still somehow of interest to men. When she died, she was already tired of her body being of interest to men. She was fourteen and slight for her age, but that didn't stop them. Did not even slow them down. You'd think death would have taken care of that.

She never learnt to read but could swear in four languages. Five, now. No accounting for it, the way certain things just keep on, banking up. An art to it. An ear. Picking up every shiny dangerous thing dropped from the mouths of canal workers, sailors, in the backstreets of her first city. An ever-expanding arsenal of savage little implements she could conceal on her small person, test the keenness of now and again. Especially on North Americans, milk-soft, with their yellow gases for killing mosquitoes, their pockets full of chewing gum and scraps for cooing strays.

She has always been fond of dogs, and dogs of her. She prefers dogs to people. If she has ever been saint to anyone or anything, it was to one mutt. Who knew what he knew, that dog. Only that when he smelled smoke he went crazy. Running around whimpering with nowhere to go. She protected him from the everyday demon of smoke. He was tiny and hurt and could not return the favor. That was all right. He let her be a kid with a dog. She rubbed the bare, pink patches on his haunches and tail, soft as she could.

For the record, it was a very popular name, in her grandmother's time, when her grandmother was a girl. In fact, it was her grandmother's name—there you have it. (Her sister has a daughter, now, and the daughter has her name. It is spoken aloud every day, many times.)

In her first city, girls her age and younger grew accustomed to the rasp of fresh stubble. Or no, not accustomed to, never really accustomed to: familiar with. Men still shaved, wanted to look respectable to fuck a child. Some girls had tricks to make themselves less girl, less appealing. Wearing their brothers' clothes, for instance. Letting their hair hang in rank snakes, or hacking it away altogether. Walking like maybe they had something you didn't want to catch. Acting wild, plain crazy. She herself was famous at crazy, convincing, bugging her eyes and twitching her limbs and swearing in her several bad languages at imaginary devils whenever a stranger approached. She might have been an actress, might have got around the world that way.

But it happened to her anyhow.

* * *

Her sister once told her that every woman who dies like that has already dreamed her death.

And girls?

Girls too. The smart ones.

She was smart. Smarter than most. Had she dreamed her death, then, or one like it? She must have. Stories of that kind went around all the time.

For a time, it had looked like she might yet survive it.

But after it happened. After that happened. Well, after that happens, some said, almost better to die sweet than to live, and grow bitter. They'd seen women grow bitter after living through a thing like that, and no, it was not a pretty sight. It bled your heart. A waste of womanhood, a sinful waste. Better to die sweet, and stay that way.

Death had not sweetened her. It had only enraged her. In death, she grew ever more enraged. The things they'd costumed her in. A joke. A joke and a lie—never in life had she worn anything so elaborately suffocating. Or hideous. Or impractical. If she had been caught going around alive in this froth, someone would have slapped her. Right down from off her high horse. And she hadn't gone into the vault that way, either. Not to begin with. No one had seen the cause for that kind of extravagance. Of course they hadn't.

Incorruptible. Who'd have guessed. (No one, that's who.)

That her body did not corrupt was not miraculous. It was perverse. That her flesh did not retain any trace of violence was a betrayal. It was absolution—she knew about absolution, what and whom it was really for—and if it had been up to her, she would not have given it. If it had been up to her, she would have rained fire and much worse upon that man and all men like him. Called all the ants down from the anthills. Made it slow. If it had been up to her.

* * *

It was a curse in some places, some parts of the world: May the earth not eat you.

In older—better—stories, no one is forgiven, and the girl escapes by becoming a tree. A laurel, or a poplar. Or a star. Even a stone—she could settle for being stone. People once believed that stones could grow, and why not? Limestone was just life heaped up on life heaped up on life and then pressed down hard over millennia. And after all that, people come along and mine it to the surface and grind it to powder and sprinkle it around again in order to call forth more life.

It's a long process. But if you could learn to think in mountain-time, it might come to seem very simple. But people are mostly stupid, very sentimental, very attached to their human time. And even mountains can be annihilated in a matter of puny human years, their insides quarried away for this or for that so in the end they collapse like an old crushed fedora. In the end, it's best not to get too attached, to dogs or mountains, anything at all.

Why not die of yellow fever, like everyone else? Then at least she might have found some peace.

There might still be time to become a tree. If offered a choice, she would prefer tree. Her tree-self would be the kind with poisonous spines that only certain birds and animals could negotiate, and whose fruits appeal only to bats. Needless to mention the armies of fierce stinging ants that would shelter in her limbs and be under her dominion.

MONDAY

by JOSEPH EARL THOMAS

SHANE WAS A HACK. He'd be flailing at anybody coming down at half court, whacking off glasses, tearing open white tees and grappling for the ball haphazardly, like a child, then calling first from the concrete outside MLK Elementary, where we always played ball from ten to two on Mondays. Those three or four hours of midday dialysis heaven where, after dropping off patients at DaVita around the corner, it was unlikely dispatch would hit you up for anything else till they were done, because you were just too far away from everything. Perhaps some calculation about gas and pay per patient. There were, of course, conformists who caught up on falsifying their paperwork around that time, following a checklist in which everyone—walking, crawling, flying or dying was a "medical necessity"—because Medicare was buckling down on reimbursement, and the profit margins, I'd supposed, for the mostly Russian owned private ambulance companies had thereafter taken a hit. StarCare would not, have our boss Boris tell it, go the way of Emergent Health or MedStar or First Response, circling the drain and hiring more or less unqualified persons for nine dollars an hour to catch and release your momma and them from condemned houses or fifth floor walk-ups two to three times a week, depositing them in white rooms with wide chairs so their blood could be sifted through a giant techno-kidney filter and forced back into their aching bodies. Certainly, there were few successful transplants.

So every Monday real ones ran full at the in-between times, packing their ambulances onto the sidewalk and hopping out with fish over rice and lamb gyros from the halal truck, happy to get beat down by Shane, who was more than happy to oblige. Shane was my partner, I should say, at least on Mondays. A great EMT otherwise, but when we stepped on the court everybody looked at me like I was responsible for him. All that "get your boy" shit. It was a tradeoff though, because Shane wasn't afraid to lift and could drive and treat folks fairly without constant intervention by me. Shane had the sight; the most experienced medic should, of course, run triage, but we were all at the same level barring the fact that Shane seemed more invested in his job as a job and not just survival. Even back in Iraq he was more consistent than most with fairness and protocol; he'd once left two guys from our unit to die while saving the life of our interpreter who was, by all accounts, higher priority given the situation. For this reason there were folks who threw shade at Shane, but this lent a kind of levity to our fourteen hour days together. Even if Shane was ugly, and a little awkward. Besides, Kareem and Ryan and them were always begging to be partnered with new women; suddenly no one minded training folks when Nya or Nabilah showed up, the latter with thick braids hanging down and resting on the top of her ass. Lise had already quit by then for a hospital gig, and so half the time Ryan and Nabilah would use their downtime to fuck, and Kareem, rejected, would play Nintendo Switch games while Nya read short stories or talked on the phone, when she wasn't making fun of folks' hoop game or lack thereof.

She followed the ball up and down court like a coach, calling Ryan's handle corny, making stank faces toward Kareem's dicked sneakers, and saying "Go head little white boy!" every time Shane got his big sloppy hands on the ball. He was a mulatto, but this was North Philly. And we were winning, or better yet, "Bussin that ass," as Nya kept saying that day. This wasn't just because Shane was on my team, but I do take some responsibility for what happened. A few new guys were there who didn't respect Shane's jump shot; he was one of those dudes that brought the ball back so comically far behind his head that everybody would laugh; my man's shot had no arc neither, just tossing it at the rim without a spec of vertical intention and the velocity of a minor league pitcher; but he was practiced and, despite the obvious lack of form, he was drainin em. This could only go on five or six times though before the other team's laughter turned to "Man, somebody stick this nigga, fuck is yall doing?!" and some poor soul would sprint out to the three point line on his over-thirty-ambulance-sitting-post-military-stressed-patient-lifting knees to no avail, either too late to catch the release, or too unaware that I was already breaking toward the rim and an easy layup because they'd also thought, up to then, that Shane couldn't pass. On one such occasion, feeling myself a little too much I guess, I forgot what those bucket rims felt like on raw flesh and cocked the ball back so far for a dunk I might have been sixteen again, for just a moment floating there in a completely legal and sanctified mode of domination through which I could dispense all manner of verbal abuses afterward, letting go of not just the politeness ordered by low-paying public facing jobs but every sleight suffered by less powerful loved ones since Phillis Wheatley was brought from Africa to America, since R. Kelly did what he did, and that social worker took both your siblings but not you, no, not you, took them both off to a better place your wages will never permit you to travel even if you *could* get off work; I took all of that and then some and shoved it down the throats of other black boys in the form of an indoor-outdoor orange inflatable rubber ball against a netless bucket rim. And missed. The ball bounced out and my wrist slammed all the harder against the enemy. And just then we heard a *pop.*

Nya stopped mid-sentence in describing that last play as everybody stood still to listen on. "Fuck was that?" she said, for no real reason, since the startle was one of familiarity and not at all of newness or true confuzzlement.

My wrist ached, but I listened in too as I held it. *Pop. Pop.* It echoed into the schoolyard at irregular beats. *Pop.* And the more it sounded, the quieter we all got, all the easier to hear them screaming through the concrete and metal barricade of the schoolhouse.

The worst thing about dead children is the unfunniness. That redeemable quality of tragedy is made unavailable, even in the subjunctive. My friends who joke about their abortions incessantly, yeeting fetuses at twenty-four weeks into buckets and strolling off with a smile of relief, or those dudes who threaten to skull fuck people's kids on *Halo,* and even some of those subjects, the all too many, who find comic relief years after being beaten bloody by prison guards and shoved into solitary confinement are all brought to sincerity upon the pulse-absent corpse of a child.

The doors weren't even locked. Best guess is they were about to come out for recess despite a heat index that may as well have said Sahara Desert at noon. I discovered this information by the fact that there was a brown corduroy wearing teacher leaned against the door, whose back had been pierced by three bullets; three separate *pop*s had terminated forevermore his dedication to America's youth or otherwise frustration with caging a gaggle of violent little crumb snatchers all day every day for poverty wages. I gleaned this from his brown corduroys, which to me have always been the symbol par excellence of a dedicated male teacher who is also, depending on the neighborhood, a substitute father. Another teacher, or maybe a teaching assistant, a blue haired woman in her twenties, lay wheezing on a rainbow area rug next to a cubby where children's shoes should go. Stupidly, we ran, without thinking about much except the wheezing woman, a paragon of the sucking chest wound this woman was, blood soon displacing the air in her lungs and activating the Pavlovian response engrained through medic school; we were all enrolled autonomically into a pulse throbbing competition to fix it. The moment I touched her, that old cartoonish screaming of the drill sergeants rang straight through my bones.

"Fuck is you doin doc! What you scared?" they yelled, squirting fake blood onto our hands, half gloved and so slippery and struggling to open the HyFin chest seals we'd saved and stored in our cargo pockets or the small soft tops of our aid bags for just such an occasion. Gunfire. Explosions. Smoke. And blown out cars with flashing red lights, white lights, streetlights blinking behind and all around us. It was not an environment for sight or sound, but for feeling, which is what too many of us got wrong on our first few runs. You need to shut up, close your eyes and practice, practice, practice. Muscle memory, not intellectual acumen, or the pontificating we were so fond of, having entered into military training with a sense of superiority over those grunts with low ASVAB scores. "What. Are. You. Doing?" the drill sergeants said. "Don't you even care? Is this too hard? Is life too fucking difficult right now you selfish piece of shit. Look at your patient dying! Do you understand what will happen if you don't get a fucking grip?" More blood squirted at us from a ketchup bottle. "Do something! Look at them all dying!"

Trembling, as I always trembled whenever someone was dying and I felt responsible—even on the news—I struggled to reposition the blue haired woman. Nya came and sliced the woman's clothes off, tossing a hand over her wound as I dried her off and closed the opening as best I could; Ryan dragged the woman off afterwards; back and forth before I could gather a true sense of what was happening, he and Nabilah had been snatching up limp children from the floor too, who seemed to continuously appear, and tossing them into their ambulance. There must have been piles of them, far too many children to have hailed from a single elementary school, *or to have died on a single day*, I thought, wrongly, lazily for a second; I knew, as much as folks refused to know, that children were slaughtered with near impunity day-in-day-out; they starved, were raped or bombed or otherwise beaten for discipline by their owners or legal guardians, parents or de facto disciplinarians, deputized by differences in age and anger; we all watched, and scraped their corpses for whatever rhetoric we might need, which for those of our generation began with the long-standing collaborations between UNICEF and mass projections of Africa, Catholic hymns, or "In the Arms of an Angel" in one long conflation between the flies colliding with wide-open eyeballs and homeless German shepherds who, if not adopted, their eyes say, have nowhere else to turn but the police. Their figure, the children, under threat and imperiled, was the guiding force beneath all the world's formal persuasion and perhaps it felt more true that there were just not enough of them cut off from the calculated illiteracy-to-labor-force-pipeline by early maiming and termination protocols and that there should have been more of them, many more short and pre-wrinkled fingers lapsed in blood, many more popped-out baby eye sockets or prepubescent vivisections, such that we might see the insides with some reflection, and what was happening could transcend, in form at the very least, from a Monday afternoon into the status of event.

Nya lugged two children, one under each arm across the schoolyard and out to her ambulance and I remember her looking silly mid-sprint, because she was awkward and lanky and we so rarely saw her run, let alone exert herself like everyone else did on the court. I remember thinking how weird the silence was, as if sirens were in order, as if the immediacy I felt personally should have the everlasting effect of rocking the foundations of the world. But I knew it did not; I also knew that was how it felt and I wished we could have still been playing ball. The kids should have been playing ball. And I wished I knew where Shane was in that very moment, till he whisked past me and down a narrow hall away from the classroom, past hand paintings of turkeys and sketched out capital letters hanging on the wall, flapping papers where children had once connected the dots on numbers one to ten, sloppily.

Shane looked goofy hooping, but not running. His run was a matter of seriousness, and he stopped only for brief seconds, checking a brown child's pulse and moving on. Checking a blond child's pulse and moving. Checking an ugly little child's pulse and moving on. Moving. The children piled up out of tune with the *pop*s. For each *pop* two children, then three, then five. Kept piling up in the room where I stood and everyone kept piling them into the ambulance and because the situation felt useless I decided to follow after Shane, who had the eye, who knew where and what needed to happen in order to reach an ending. He ran down the hall. I ran after him. He did not stop for pieces of children; we could not waste the time. He sprinted over them, stepping on two hands and one twisted little spine and toward the echo of another *pop*. Down the hall to where, it seemed, all echoes originated. *Pop.* There was no air-conditioning, and it was muggy. My glasses fogged. Another *pop*. Shane stumbled to a tripod, short of breath, then to a knee and tried to get back up. *Pop.* I slipped on the floor and struggled to get back up too, wiping my glasses all the while. A beady eyed boy with an Eagles fitted stood there over Shane, trembling, as if someone was dying and he felt responsible; he was terrified about responsibility, and kept pulling the trigger because the empty click of doing something was better than doing nothing, and people were dying, he could see, and he needed to make something happen, and for fear, for freedom, that is precisely what he could do; he had made something happen. If he just kept pulling the trigger enough we would all be swept up by a wave strong enough to rock the bureaucratic centers of the earth. And together, we got used to the clicking sound of an empty chamber; we would miss it when it was gone, and at our best we would dream the sound and remember the feeling, the clicking, the popping, the sweat and musk and piling and how we needed, above all, to feel like something could happen.

SCALA 40

by VALERIA PARRELLA

Translated from the Italian by Sonya Gray Redi

I.

AT 5:25 P.M. ON August 31 Vera awoke and remembered her dream. It was the dream about the heron. A month had passed since they'd arrived at the campground, and she'd already dreamed it five times, but this was the first time she remembered doing so.

She was thirteen years old when she first saw the heron. It was the only one she'd ever seen in her life. Overgrown and deformed, it laboriously tried to flap its wings without ever taking flight.

She opened her eyes and turned onto her side. She watched the flies outside the window screen and sensed that the dream was bad, that it had hurt her, so she counted the flies, and mentally calculated the time it would take to repack all her clothes. Numbers came easily to her and relaxed her. If only she'd thought of it twenty years ago, she would've pursued mathematics. But she didn't think of it and married her husband instead.

He was next to her now: a man who managed to make noise even without snoring. That afternoon they'd had sex, during which at one point Vera had looked at her leg and gotten distracted: from then on, she'd thought of other things.

The bungalow's stovetop was on the veranda. Vera made coffee while watching her son approach from the pine grove. There was no doubt: she didn't know him, he didn't belong to her, he'd never belonged to her. She loved her children because that distance was what they called love.

"Ma, I'm taking a shower."

If she hadn't been remembering her dream, she would've told him not to come in so sandy.

She'd seen the heron on a field trip: twelve hours later she'd gotten her first period. It had flown away leaving a pink trail in the air. For the next ten years, she'd dragged that heron into her dreams, and at some point, it always took off and vanished, like it had in real life.

But since she'd gotten pregnant with Giulia, she had no longer dreamed it. And now that she'd turned forty it had reappeared, during this vacation.

Vera watched her daughter grow; she found it easier to reflect on her than on herself. She was the mother of a sixteen-year-old girl without knowing how. The fact astounded her still, much like it had sixteen years prior.

She set her espresso cup down and reached for the cards. The last game of the season was scheduled for 6:30 p.m. She shuffled, flipped thirty-four cards, and repeated to herself the missing ones.

"What's wrong?" her husband asked as he took her ankle and placed it on his lap.

"I had a bad dream."

"Oh, Giulia! Your mother had a bad dream. I bet you she'll lose today!"

Vera laughed: for the last decade she'd won thirty days in a row every year. Giulia had been six and Luca three—that day they had followed twenty-six ants in a line to their ant farm.

"Where do they go now, Mom?" Luca had asked.

"To sleep," she'd answered. If she'd thought of it at the time, she could've invented a better story, but she didn't think of it.

She spent the next thirty-five minutes in the bathroom. She dried the floor, which was still wet from Luca's shower, picked up his clothes, and undressed.

She trimmed her nails. They grew two millimeters a week without her having to think about it. She rubbed her body in coconut oil, then dried herself only a little in order to keep her skin glistening.

She tied her hair back, put on a nice bathing suit that she could never have worn at the beach, and covered it with a sarong. It took her fifteen minutes. Then she sat on the toilet lid and stayed for thirty.

She stared at each of the tiles.

She heard the voices of Sandra and Dario, who were arriving for the game, so she peed, and her urine was dotted with stains from her early menopause.

"You're not pregnant, ma'am. You're starting menopause way earlier than average," her doctor had said.

"Even better," she'd replied.

It took some effort for her to get up, for she felt the weight of the heron in her legs. So she decided to abandon that dream there, and flushed.

That afternoon, Dario had touched himself in the bathroom thinking of Vera, so he now watched her shuffle cards with a complicity typically reserved for bedmates. So did her husband.

Giulia attended the game of Scala 40, for it was the last of the season. After three rounds her mother felt confident so she winked at her: Giulia laughed and the rest of the table grew nervous.

Vera closed her fan of cards and looked at her hands—she hadn't painted her nails in years, would only ever add a clear coat. The first time she'd painted them, her mother had slapped her. If she had thought of it back then, she could've asked her if she loved her. But she didn't think of it. Besides, the answer would have been *Of course!* That slap was what they called love.

She counted in her mind the cards that hadn't been drawn yet. One or the other could turn up, but none of them would have truly surprised her. Nothing surprised her more than finding herself forty years old sitting at that table with a husband next to her, two children near, and a heron that had reappeared in her dreams. The rest of the group laid their cards on the table; they took and traded while she lit a cigarette. She counted her forty points backward and forward once more; as soon as she finished smoking, she laid them down all together, year after year.

They'd been expecting it. Her husband smacked a kiss on her hand; they did the math.

Vera turned toward the vacated campground and saw a gypsy walking toward them. She'll stop and read my cards, Vera thought: she'll find a calling higher than destiny's and will read it aloud. That way I'll be able to get up, everyone will rush to hand me a suitcase, a hat, and cigarettes—*Hurry*, they'll say.

That evening Vera counted in the sink seventy-two clams in need of cleaning for the last peppered clam dish.

2.

Her husband lit his first cigarette just as the table next to them asked for their bill. Vera was listening to them without turning her head:

they must have been about fifteen years old, and at 2:20 p.m. they'd already finished eating their pizzas. Thirty-four fifty. Her husband didn't notice. Coming in, he'd taken his usual spot in front of the television. It was muted, so now any meaning could be gleaned only by staring at it. They'd already known his order: two calzoni, a small Peroni, and a bottle of mineral water. Then the first cigarette.

Thirty-four fifty divided by six kids is five seventy-five, which, if they rounded up to six euros each, would leave one fifty for the waiter. But maybe at fifteen you don't leave a tip.

Perhaps her daughter, Giulia, was also getting up from a table like this one.

"After school next Saturday we're going out for pizza with some seniors."

"Do you have an in?" sniped Luca.

"We don't need one. So, Mami, is it okay?"

Okay then. If she'd thought about it, she could have asked her a thing or two about those seniors. But she didn't think of it, and Giulia glued herself to her phone.

"Mom, the seniors won't go out with them unless they've got an in."

Vera couldn't understand why Luca wouldn't drop it, until he said, "Saturday afternoon I'd like to watch the Grand Prix with Andrea. His mom said I could eat with them."

So he'd created a distraction. The ins and outs of his sister's romantic life had diverted attention from his request.

As a result, a new day of the week was assigned to her: a Saturday to go out, eat out. The kids weren't there, moreover, they did as they pleased. Like Vera, who also did as she pleased. She lifted her hair in front of the mirror, tying it up in order to show off her tan shoulders for as long as she could, because it was the end of September, after all, the heat was brutal, and if you weren't careful the sweat would cause your clothes to adhere.

The husband looked at her, smiled, put out his cigarette, and poured his beer into his glass. He had a beautiful wife whose legs he could touch under the table, and he'd get home in time for the Grand Prix.

Vera observed her husband's hand caressing her left knee, then she glanced at her feet leaning up against the wooden bar of the chair, and beneath her feet, at ground level, she saw her dead calm flow by.

It spread on the floor like mist does in the country, traversing the tiles in the direction of the oven.

The teens had done the division on a cell phone, and now found themselves with not enough money to give the waiter.

"But I did it on my phone!"

"Listen, miss, you can do it wherever you want, but you owe me thirty-four fifty."

Vera turned around. "It's five seventy-five each."

The teens recognized the authority of a Neapolitan mother over that of Japanese technology and stuck their hands back into their wallets.

Amused, the waiter smiled and unabashedly looked at her legs.

Once the kids had left, they said something to one another, after which Vera decided that her chair wobbled too much so got up to switch it.

"It's not the chair, ma'am. It's the floor."

So her husband gave her his spot, and as the waiter held out the chair for her, Vera realized, as did the waiter, that her dress clung to her thighs.

The calzoni arrived, and each was exactly the diameter of a pizza folded in half. Her husband grabbed one with a paper napkin and took the first bite. Vera thought about how she'd ironed that shirt before coming down, that ironing a shirt required twenty minutes of ironing at 140 degrees, and said, "Use a fork and knife, or you'll get dirty."

Only thirteen years had passed. Giulia was three, Vera was seven months pregnant, and they were transforming a love story into a marriage.

"Use a fork and knife, or you'll get dirty," she'd told her husband.

He had recognized that advice as legitimate and had confused, that time and forever since, his woman with a mother, with a sister, with the woman who would birth his second child. He had placed the profiterole on the plate and wiped off his fingers. If only Vera had thought of it, she could've smiled, but she didn't think of it.

The waiter had gone looking for solidarity from the cashier and pizzaiolo—that woman was driving him crazy. Now she'd lit herself a cigarette. He couldn't bear to look at her, yet he was dying to bring her the check. In the end he brought it to her husband, but found the money already counted on the table, with a tip on the side.

Vera gazed out the street-facing window as her husband finished off his cigarette while staring at the TV. What had been different about that Saturday was about to end.

On the way out, Vera said goodbye to the waiter, then instantly looked down at the floor. He felt his discomfort laid bare and thought he had embarrassed her. But Vera was watching her dead calm envelop her steps.

3.

She didn't need an alarm. She had an internal clock, precise to the very second, which woke her the minute she'd decided. And if she hadn't decided, it woke her in time to remind her of what she'd dreamed.

She drank her first coffee while everyone slept. It was something that was solely hers, a slice of the world revealed only to her.

Then she'd turn on the space heater in the bathroom so she could wash herself when it was cold. Her husband would give her a boiler for Christmas that year.

"Mom, are you done yet?"

"Come in, look."

"At your forehead?"

"This wrinkle. I didn't have it yesterday."

"Yeah, move it."

"Does it look normal to you?"

"Grab your cream and leave me the bathroom."

That morning, which wasn't a normal morning, the sky was gray, everyone was making a mess looking for things to put on, and no one rinsed their milk cup. That morning Vera discovered her new wrinkle: a question mark that started from her eyebrow and outlined her cheekbone until her cheek.

If she'd thought of it, she could've asked her husband for an explanation, asked him why that particular shape and why her. But she didn't think of it, and her husband left for work.

"I never work in the mornings. We don't open before noon. Only the pizzaiolo is there, to turn on the oven."

"I'll stop by at nine thirty, then."

The space heater consumed a ton of energy. It'd take ten minutes and two thousand watts just to warm a fifty-square-foot bathroom.

The night before, Vera had locked herself in that bathroom to shave. Her husband was having trouble: she'd asked him to make sure that the oven didn't go over four hundred degrees, but he hadn't paid attention, and now wished to remedy it, but the oven could no longer be opened, if not the pizza would have collapsed.

They spoke through the bathroom door. Vera was getting ready for her appointment with surgical precision: she liked to depilate the night before so her skin's redness would have time to fade. The hair removal cream stayed on for ten minutes. In ten minutes, the space heater transformed the bathroom into an oven, the oven cooked two-thirds of the pizza, and a razor could shave two armpits.

The bathroom door split Vera in two: held within were her body, heat, and sensuality; outside the door stood her husband with an oven mitt, and she directed him like she was directing the razor blade along the curve of her groin. It was like she was directing a concert, because even without seeing it, she knew full well how a half-baked pizza was.

Then she hopped into the shower.

She went downstairs at 8:50 a.m. and tried to flatten her wrinkle in the elevator: it ironed itself out a little, but as soon as her hand released it, it went back to asking questions. To anyone who, unlike her family, wasn't in a hurry, it would've been plainly obvious that the wrinkle did not have a normal shape.

She turned onto Via Settembrini, bought groceries, looked at her reflection in every store window, studied the fruit grocer's eyes upon the question mark, then walked beneath the arch of Saint Gennaro's Gate, and already there on that big street, no one knew her anymore.

She buzzed and he answered immediately. Standing in the lobby by herself, she set the grocery bags down for a minute. Then she picked them back up and started climbing the stairs.

She was going up to the third floor and every floor had two ramps with ten stairs each. Vera ascended and thirty years passed by, thirty-one, nearly thirty-five. Vera had been dragged up and down stairs, off to places she wouldn't have chosen. Whenever she felt like she had nothing that was solely hers, she started counting things. She discovered that the decorations within marble steps were done diagonally, between those squares that everyone saw; she found numbers wedged into places adults didn't look. And that symmetry was a slice of the world revealed only to her.

At the top of the stairs, he came toward her.

For Vera, a man greeting her at the door was a new, beautiful thing.

"How are you?"

"Out of breath."

"If you'd told me you had groceries, I would've come down to help."

She smiled.

They loved one another all morning: at one point, Vera looked at her leg and got distracted. From then on, she thought of other things.

COLD SUMMER

by T. C. BOYLE

I GOT IN THE habit of turning on all four burners of the stove in the morning and leaving them on till the house began to warm up, if only to the point where it was just bearable. We would have bundled up and sat out on the terrace in the sun, but there was no sun, and day after day the sky just shone white, like a blank sheet of paper. Frost killed everything we planted—corn, peas, tomatoes, even zucchini—and in the woods out back of the house the buds of the trees blackened and died and grew back and died again. It snowed three inches on the Fourth of July.

We were in the kitchen one morning, sipping coffee, paging through twice-read newspapers, and waiting for the snow to melt. My wife, Melinda, pushed herself up from the table. "Jesus, I'm bored," she said. "I think I'm going to go into town. We need anything? Beyond the usual, I mean?"

"Milk," I said. "Cheese, yogurt, maybe some salad mix. Tomatoes, if they've got them, because we're sure as hell not going to be
growing any here, not this year, anyway."

"And wine? How're we on wine?"

"You can never have too much."

She was dressed in a pair of faded thermals, over which she'd pulled
her cut-off blue jeans. I liked the way her legs looked climbing up
out of her boots and I liked her red puffer jacket too, which was close-
fitting and stylish, but also served the practical purpose of warning off
the hunters when we went for walks in the fall. We'd put our winter
gear away during a warm spell in April, but then we'd had no choice
but to dig it all out again. July, and I was sitting at the kitchen table
in a goose-down vest with a knit cap pulled over the tips of my ears.
It was beyond unusual, especially since the previous summer had been
the hottest on record worldwide and some seven thousand people had
died of heat-related causes in the US and Canada alone. Still, the way
I saw it—and Melinda did too—it was better to shiver than sweat,
and with the freak snow we didn't have to worry about wildfires. So
the weather had gone schizophrenic—what else was new?

I lingered over my coffee, listening to her footsteps as she tapped
down the hallway, lifted her purse from the coat tree, and pulled the
front door shut behind her. I had nothing special planned for the day—
that was the beauty of retirement—but I envisioned working my way
through various chores in the house and yard and eventually winding
up on the couch with a book in hand and the quilt pulled up to my
chin. I was just about to get up and put the breakfast dishes in the sink
when I heard the front door slam and Melinda's footsteps coming back
up the hallway. I assumed she'd forgotten something, but that wasn't it.

"The car won't start," she announced. "Again."

The car was a Swedish Olfputt, pricey but stalwart and with the
best range of any EV on the market, and we kept it plugged in 24-7.

The problem, of course, was that it wasn't charging, because the sun had all but disappeared. "All we need is a sunny day or two," I said, and as I said it I noticed that the stove's burners were no longer glowing and the LED display on the clock radio had faded to black. And no, we weren't on the grid and we didn't have a backup system either, because the house, which we'd designed ourselves, was 100 percent self-sufficient, the entire east-, south-, and west-facing portions of the roof arrayed with solar panels, the windows double-paned, and everything sealed tight with the newest and stingiest vacuum insulation. In the basement, where older homes might feature an obscenely wasteful fuel-oil furnace, we'd set up an array of the best lithium-ion batteries money could buy.

She had her hands on her hips, giving me a look I didn't like, as if all this was my fault. "I said from the beginning we needed a generator for times like these."

"But there were never times like these, not till now, anyway."

"My point exactly."

I wanted to say that generators and furnaces were pollution bombs that only made things worse vis-à-vis the warming that was crippling the planet and killing people in their own bedrooms and living rooms and kitchens, but she'd already swung round and started back down the hall. "I'm taking my bike," she called over her shoulder.

"But it's fifteen miles. The roads are icy. It's dangerous."

"I need to get out," she said, and then the door slammed and she was gone.

There's a pattern to events in our lives that's only recognizable after the fact, a concatenation of steps or missteps that leads to the major incident—the crowning incident—revealing the warp and woof of things that dictate the circumstances, whether we're prepared for them or not. Melinda was halfway to town when a pickup going the other way threw up a wall of slush and she lost control and went down hard on the pavement, fracturing her right tibia and the two lower ribs on that side, the floating ribs, as they're commonly known because they're attached not to the sternum but to the spine itself. If the sun had been shining the way it was supposed to in the month of July, the car would have been fully charged and my wife would have taken it to town, avoiding the bike, the slush, the pickup truck. But because there was no sun, there was no electricity and no functioning automobile and thus my wife found herself sprawled on the shoulder of the road, wet and cold and gritting her teeth against the pain while the driver of the pickup, oblivious, vanished into the whitish blur of the horizon. And more, and worse: her cell phone had no charge, so even if she could have gotten it out of her pocket despite the blinding pain, it wouldn't have mattered. There isn't a whole lot of traffic on that road—we built out here with the intention of getting away from the crush of humanity—so she lay there for something like forty-five minutes before she managed to flag down a car, and the driver, whose cell was fully charged because he was on the grid, could call 911 and the ambulance could make its racketing way to her.

I knew nothing of this, of course. My own phone was dead too. There was no milk for the homemade granola I usually had for lunch, because the refrigerator was down like everything else in the house and I didn't like the smell of what was left in the carton. I made a peanut butter sandwich and washed it down with tap water, then spent the afternoon trimming the arborvitae hedge out front. I was just finishing up when a strange car turned in to the driveway. There was a woman I didn't recognize behind the wheel and Melinda was sitting beside her. The sky darkened. Pellets of sleet began to rattle down.

As it turned out, the woman was one of the nurses from the regional hospital, who lived out on Route 22 and was kind enough to give Melinda a lift on her way home from work. I had no idea what was going on, but I dropped the clippers in confusion when the passenger door swung open and I got my first look at my wife in her altered condition, a cast on one leg and a pair of gleaming aluminum crutches thrust over the seat back like parentheses framing her head. "She's had an accident," the nurse said, redundantly. In the next moment we were both helping my wife in through the front door and onto the couch because she was in no shape to negotiate the stairs to the bedroom.

The nurse, who lived just five miles and two junctions up the road, though we'd never met her or even seen her before as far as I knew, filled me in on the details, doing most of the talking because Melinda was pretty well drugged-up. At one point I offered her a cup of tea but was frustrated there since neither the stove nor microwave was functioning. I thought of the outdoor gas grill we used for barbecuing, but that was more effort than I was willing to expend under the circumstances.

Melinda, her bad leg elevated and her head thrown back against the cushions, began to snore with a soft rasp and gargle before I could rescind my offer of tea. Not that it mattered. The nurse was already on her feet and excusing herself in a blizzard of instructions regarding my wife's care and the doling out of the medications she was handing me in their sealed plastic tubes. I barely heard her. I was watching Melinda, her suffering face, the awkward way she'd arranged her limbs, the cast, the bit of fluff caught in her hair I realized must have been a memento of the stiffened weeds along the roadway, and then we were at the door. I thanked the nurse, whose name I never did catch, and then, because I couldn't think of anything else to say, I made a comment on the conditions that had brought us—two strangers—to this valedictory moment on a bitter unseasonable July day in the front hall of my house. "This weather, huh? Ever seen anything like it?"

The nurse, her eyes in escape mode and the white pleats of her uniform knifing away from a blue quilted jacket that was two sizes too big for her, paused in the doorway and gave me a look. "They're saying it's the Russians."

"The Russians? What are you talking about?"

"They shot up some satellite or something. It's all over the news."

The information was so confounding, so fraught (and, as it turned out, wrong, but not by all that much), that I didn't think to ask to borrow her cell till it was too late and her car had already swung out onto the main road. If I'd thought of it in time, I could have called Triple A and had someone come tow the car to a charging station, after which I'd drive directly to the first store I could find that carried generators. It was just past four in the afternoon. My wife was on the couch, in pain. Every breath I took hung like a shroud in front of my face. There was nothing I could do short of starting a signal fire on the lawn, which most likely nobody would have been able to see from the road in any case, so I went back to check on Melinda—still asleep—and continued on out to the deck and lit the grill. I was thinking I'd heat up a couple cans of soup and serve them with crackers and red wine—a California Cab I'd been saving for a special occasion, and this, it seemed to me, was as special as an occasion could get.

In the morning, which hung in the bedroom window like a wet sheet, Melinda seemed better, or at least more alert. I woke her at seven or so, helped her to the bathroom (the crutches took some getting used to, as I knew from personal experience), then made us eggs and toast on the outdoor grill, with mixed results, the eggs sticking to the pan and the toast singed around the edges till it took on the color of the scorched ceramic stones in the depths of the thing. We ate on the couch in the living room, Melinda with her broken leg thrust out at an odd angle, as if it belonged to somebody else.

"How are you feeling?" I asked.

"Cold," she said. "Beyond that? Shitty. Really shitty. What luck, huh?"

I murmured a consolatory phrase or two, but I wasn't fully there—I was mentally paging through the handbook of how to get us out of this predicament. "I thought I'd try walking up to the neighbors' place and see if I could use their phone to call Triple A— would you be okay with that? I wouldn't be gone long..."

"What neighbors? You don't mean what's-their-name, do you? The ones that can't even bother to wave when they see us sitting right there on the porch?"

The nearest neighbors, the Zinssers, had moved into the old farmhouse half a mile up the hill in back of us, a house buried so deep in the forest you couldn't catch even a glimpse of it from our property. They were unsmiling people, unfriendly, and we'd never exchanged more than ten words with them. "You have a better plan? It's an emergency, okay? If I don't get the car going, if we can't call anybody, or what, buy food even..." I trailed off. Wasn't it obvious?

It was a ten-minute walk. The leaves drooped on the trees. I didn't see a single animate thing, not a bird or squirrel or even an insect, and I wondered about that, about nature and how the freak weather was affecting natural rhythms—the birds could have flown back down south, I supposed, but the squirrels didn't have all that many options, and if the oaks and hickories didn't recover, there'd be precious little for them to rely on when winter, true winter, came round. It was strange. And depressing.

The Zinssers' house needed paint. Their car—a gas-guzzling SUV in a color that might once have been red—stood in the driveway like a relic of another time, which it was. The house had a slate roof topped by a chimney that was currently in use, expelling smoke. I crossed the yard, mounted the front steps, and knocked on the door. There was no response. I knocked again. Still nothing. Finally, a hand flicked back the curtains—Mrs. Zinsser's—and what was her name, anyway, Josie or Gerry or something like that? Her eyes seized on me. There was the sound of the bolt turning in the lock and then the door pulled back three inches on its chain, which remained fastened, and there was her face, rucked and seamed and unsmiling and no older than my own. "What do you want?" she demanded, without preliminary.

As I stood there explaining myself, a seep of warmth drifted through the crack of the door, along with the scent of something baking—bread, I thought it was, or dinner rolls. My glands clenched. "My husband's not here," she said.

"That's okay, not a problem, I just wonder if I could use your phone a minute—"

"Sorry," she said.

"Or an outlet." I held up my phone, as useless without a charge as a shiny stone I'd picked up along the roadway. "Could I just plug it in long enough to get a charge and call Triple A?"

"I'm sorry," she said, and the door eased shut.

Was this maddening? Of course it was. We hadn't asked for neighbors in the first place, but really, what was the use of them if you couldn't even count on them in an emergency? And this was an emergency, no mistake about it—and not just for us, as I was soon to discover, but everybody on the planet. I wound up pleading at the door for I don't know how long, and then, getting no response, I let out a curse and kicked the lower panel—twice, as hard as I could—before giving up and heading back down the road. I didn't stop in at the house, because I couldn't face giving my wife the bad news or debating over my determination to walk the fifteen miles to town, bad knee notwithstanding.

There was no traffic on the main road. It was cold. My knee hurt. The day flickered around me. I must have walked three or four miles before a car appeared, and though it was going in the opposite direction and I felt humiliated by my need and the obliviousness— stupidity—that had brought me to this pass, I waved my arms and jerked my thumb at the face behind the windshield even as the car gathered speed and blew right past me. I've had two surgeries on my right knee and I suffer from occasional bouts of plantar fasciitis, and I really don't think I would've made it, if finally—maybe five miles in—a car hadn't stopped for me. The driver was a teenager, his hair piled atop his head in a meticulous confection designed to look windblown even when the wind wasn't blowing, and before I was halfway through my story of need and privation he cut me off. "You mean you haven't heard?"

What I hadn't heard, because of our isolation and our dead batteries and all the rest, was that the schizophrenic weather was not a result of natural causes (if anything can be called natural anymore, given human interference with the ecosystem and the relentless buildup of carbon dioxide in the atmosphere). No. The current cooling trend was attributable to a single cause, a single individual, in fact, who'd taken it on himself to turn down the thermostat on global warming sans consulting the eight billion other people collectively riding this big shining rock around the sun with him. The story had just broken that day. It was all anybody could talk about.

But let me back up a moment—have you heard of the Cold Summer of 1816, when hundreds of people died of starvation right here in New England because the sun didn't shine for months at a time? People thought it was the apocalypse, that the sun was dying and the Earth was going back to a time when glaciers rode across the land, freezing and crushing everything in their path. Crops failed. Subsistence farmers had nothing to subsist on. And it was worse, far worse, than today, because there were no supermarkets back then, no supply chains or truckers to long-haul foodstuffs all the way up from the South. As it turned out, the cause of the deep freeze wasn't a moribund sun but the eruption of Mount Tambora in the Dutch East Indies the previous year, which sent thirty-six cubic miles of gasses and debris into the atmosphere, effectively shading the Earth like a God-sized parasol. That was a natural occurrence, part of the price humanity had to pay for inhabiting a planet with a molten core, but what had happened now—no more than a month ago, as far as the authorities could determine—was an act of sabotage, pure and simple.

A Filipino billionaire no one had ever heard of, except, I suppose, Filipinos, retrofitted half a dozen corporate jets and hired pilots to fly them into the stratosphere and release droplets of sulfuric acid, which in turn combined with water vapor to form sulfate aerosols, effectively shading the Earth until such time as they should naturally dissipate, anywhere from two to three years or more. No one was certain. Nor was anyone certain about the *amount* released or how that would affect things. There was universal outrage. The Chinese threatened war (but with whom, that was the question—the Philippines?). Democrats applauded—finally, something was being done about climate change—but Republicans were violently opposed, at least at first, until they realized that this would be a boon for the fossil fuel industry, that paid their bills and got them reelected year after sweltering year. Meanwhile, the billionaire—Bonifacio

Delossantos—was somewhere on the high seas in his two-hundred-foot superyacht and he wasn't taking any calls.

The kid didn't have all the details—I got them later, as the story deepened and expanded till it was the only story that meant anything to anybody—but the general outline was bad enough. Things weren't going to get better anytime soon. We were cold and getting colder.

I asked the kid to drop me off at the library. If there seemed to be an unusual level of activity out on the streets—cars backed up at the intersections, pedestrians everywhere, a police cruiser idling at the curb, lights slowly rotating—the library was deserted but for a pair of preteen girls giggling over a laptop at the far end of a gleaming oak table, and the sweet-faced librarian perched on a stool behind the desk, staring into space. I went directly to the nearest table, plugged in my phone, and called Triple A.

The agent who came on the line was practiced and efficient, a woman with a Southern accent that seemed incongruous under the circumstances. After congratulating me on my twenty-two-year membership in the Automobile Association, she put the essential questions to me regarding the vehicle's location, make, color, and license plate number. "Is it in a safe spot?" she asked.

"It's in my driveway," I told her. "Problem is, my driveway's fifteen miles away. Is there any way the tow truck driver could pick me up at the main library and take me back out to the house?"

"You're required to be with the vehicle when our technician arrives," she informed me.

"I understand, but you see, we're out in the countryside and I had to hitchhike into town to make this call because all our batteries are dead—with this weather, this sabotage or terrorism or whatever it is..." A pleading note had entered my voice.

"You're required to be with the vehicle when our technician arrives," she repeated.

"Right, but how am I supposed to get there?"

"Your call is very important to us," the woman said, and then the line went dead.

You might ask why I didn't call someone to come get me, but the truth is, we haven't made a whole lot of friends since we moved to the country and it really wasn't like us to solicit favors or inconvenience people (and to tell the truth, we didn't want to be inconvenienced either, which was why we'd moved in the first place). I thought of the O'Kanes—Ty and Emma, a couple we'd had over for dinner to reciprocate for their having had us over for dinner—but they were in Europe. Beyond that, it was going to have to be Uber or the local taxi service, which was an uncertain proposition at the best of times.

I stared round the room, feeling increasingly uneasy. My phone was 1 percent charged. Melinda was all alone in the house. What if she needed something? What if she got up to get a glass of water or another blanket and tripped and fell? And what about the world, how was that doing? Despite myself, I couldn't help scrolling through the news reports, though I knew it would prolong the time it would take to charge the phone, but what else was I going to do? The world's weather radically altered? How could that be? What did it mean, even? I hungered for the details, but at this juncture there was nothing but speculation and a panoply of graphs, charts, and satellite images showing the spread of the contamination round the globe. There were no riots, not yet, but there were reports of panic buying, as in any crisis, and the video feeds showed lines at the supermarkets, depleted shelves, people pushing carts piled high with toilet paper, frozen entrées, canned goods.

It took the better part of an hour for my phone to charge to 50 percent, by which time my unease had morphed into something approaching panic. I tried to picture our larder, what we had and what we lacked, and then I was on my feet and heading out the door, the two girls long gone, the librarian, head down, riveted now by her own phone. I had to get back as soon as I could, that was my all and everything, but first I made my way up the street to the Handi-Mart, where I figured I'd pick up a few essentials and then call the Uber to pick me up there in the parking lot, where I'd be easy to spot.

The first thing I noticed were the cars, a line of them snaking into the lot, which was already full to capacity, and then the glut of people at the door, a line there too. A woman emerged with a cart filled entirely with Cheetos, followed by a man with half a dozen two-liter bottles of root beer clutched to his chest. Drivers began leaning on their horns. The line at the door lurched and fell back and lurched again. I hadn't been there more than sixty seconds when I felt a tap on my shoulder and turned round on a squat man in a neon orange parka. "You on line?" he demanded. "Or you just going to stand there taking up space?"

That was enough for me—we'd just have to make do with what we had, and, of course, once I got the car charged I could always load up on whatever it was going to take to get us through this. I mumbled an apology, ducked past him, and headed back for the library. It was evening now, but since the sky was so muted it was hard to tell. In the interval the temperature had dropped even farther, the display at the bank reading twenty-three degrees, if that was accurate, and why wouldn't it be? Anything was possible now.

Urgency propelled me up the library steps, but when I tried to snatch open the door I found it locked, though the hours listed on the plaque beside it in clear, unmistakable cut-glass letters claimed it was open till eight. I felt a tick of irritation, but then I realized the librarian was probably feeling the same way I was—we all just needed to get home, that was all. I eased myself down on the steps, my feet aching, and dialed Uber. The call went right through—to a recording informing me that due to heavy volume it would be two hours to speak with a representative, and the graphic showed that there were no cars available anywhere near me. I tried Lyft. Ditto. A cab was going to be expensive—no one wanted to go all the way out in the country, even under normal conditions—but cost was no longer a consideration. Melinda needed me. That was all that mattered, period. I went through the numbers for each of the six cab companies listed but no one picked up, and when I got to voicemail I was informed that the mailboxes were full and couldn't accept any more messages. I thought then of a rental car, but the only rental cars were out at the regional airport—and that was twenty-five miles in the opposite direction.

Finally, in frustration, I crossed the street to a bar Melinda and I had been to a few times before, though at this stage in our lives bars didn't hold quite the attraction for us as when we were younger. I was starting to feel the effects of the cold and I thought maybe a shot of something would do me good—or a cognac, in a warmed snifter—till I could get through to somebody to take me home and save the day. I thought of the pipes freezing, of Melinda freezing, of the sky crashing down like a big calving ice sheet, and I pushed through the door and fell into another world.

The place was packed. All three of the TVs bracketed over the bar were showing live-feed reactions from around the globe. There were aerial shots of the billionaire's yacht heaving across a pale, deserted sea, intercut with images of crowds amassed in protest and celebration both. One woman, in close-up, sported the name DELOSSANTOS written in lipstick across her forehead, with IS inscribed on her left check and GOD on the right. I maneuvered my way up to the bar and ordered a Martell, but the bartender informed me there'd been a run on it and the best he could do was well brandy, if that was okay.

Suddenly I was sweating. My phone felt as if it had been greased. What was I doing? I needed to get out of there, get in a car, get home. "Sure," I said. And then: "Make it a double."

Time passed. The images on the screens repeated over and over, giving way briefly to various panels of breathless commentators, politicians, and religious figures—the pope, Joel Osteen, Al Sharpton—but I was enlivened by the alcohol and the simple repetitive task of calling Uber and Lyft and the six cab numbers in succession, over and over. At one point, the man I was standing elbow-to-elbow with at the bar leaned in and said, "You're going pretty hard at that thing, aren't you?"

It was as if I'd been underwater, holding my breath, swimming from one end of an Olympic pool to the other. "I'm trying to get home," I said.

The man looked to be in his fifties, hair gone white, though his eyebrows and the soul beard he sported were dark still. He was dressed in the country mode—"country casual," as they called it in the ads, flannel shirt, down vest, knit cap. "What, your car broke down?"

I told him the story, my wife laid up, the car in the driveway, dead, the house dead, nobody answering the phones anywhere. My voice caught in my throat. Unbidden, a second drink appeared right at my elbow on the slick shining surface of the bar.

He made a face, long in the jaw, his eyes narrowed to slits. "Tough luck," he said. "Jesus. And I'd really like to help you out, but—"

At which point I said, "A hundred bucks."

And he said, "Plus twenty for gas."

His name was Rutherford, and whether it was his first or last name, I never discovered. He drove a Ford pickup that sat so high off the ground I had to use both hands to lift myself into the cab. He didn't bother with his seat belt, which meant that the warning chime stayed on, chirping away, though I dutifully fastened my own. "One more nanny device," he said, wheeling away from the curb.

I hadn't succeeded in getting groceries or anything else for that matter and I was probably going to have to drain the pipes when I got back home, but I'd managed to charge the phone, even if it was only at 30 percent at this juncture, and I was on my way back to Melinda—if I was feeling the effects of the drinks on an empty stomach, chalk it up to collateral damage. I was thinking if I couldn't get hold of Triple A, I'd call the appliance place in town and have them come out and hook up a generator for us—if they had any left in stock and they did that sort of thing, that is. And maybe we'd get some sun, who knew—the stratosphere was vast, after all, and it was bound to break through at some point. Rutherford turned down a side street to avoid the traffic, then found another and another, and then we were out on the main road, drifting through the descent of night. Things were looking up. Finally.

What did we talk about? The weather. There was no other topic. It was Rutherford's opinion, based on what he'd heard on talk radio, that the Filipino billionaire didn't exist and the whole thing was a hoax cooked up by the libs to score points on the environment, a position that made no sense at all, given the fact that it was winter in July and I was a lib myself. The heater roared, the roadside crept by, the seat belt chime chimed. Rutherford drove with excessive caution—so slowly, in fact, that I kept thinking he was about to pull off on the shoulder to get out and check the tires or empty his bladder. I said, "Well, something's up—everything I planted, even the corn, was wiped out by the frost. And the trees—what about the trees?"

"Seasonal variation. You've got to look at the long term." He paused, both forearms resting on the wheel. The speedometer hovered at just under twenty miles an hour. "You a gambling man?" he asked.

I shook my head.

"Because now's the time to place your bet. Give it a month—August, you'll see. Dog days. Remember the dog days?"

I didn't respond. The last thing I wanted was to contradict him, given the circumstances. So what if he was as dense as a side of beef? So what if he was exactly the kind of person, ruled by ignorance and superstition, we'd isolated ourselves to avoid? I needed him. At least for ten or twelve miles more.

But then, without warning, he flicked on the blinker and sliced across the road and into the gravel lot of what proved to be the Pine Top Tavern, the only business between our house and town, a place we'd never visited, though it was listed in all the guidebooks as an example of an authentic New England country tavern that had been dutifully draining beer kegs for nearly two hundred years. "Is that Ginny's car?" he demanded, pointing at the rear end of a sky blue Ford Fiesta rimed with frost. "It is, isn't it?"

"Look," I said, "I really need to—" but he cut me off.

"I'll just be a minute. Truly. Just one minute."

I sat there in the dark cab of the pickup staring at the neon beer signs in the window of the bar for I don't how long, caught deep in the grip of a world I no longer recognized. If Rutherford had left the keys in the ignition I think I would have driven off and left him there, but he hadn't, because why should he trust me, a complete stranger who didn't even trust himself anymore? There were twelve cars in the lot, all of them sitting there inert, bumpers and trim faintly glowing in the pulsing neon light. Nothing moved. Nobody came out the door or wheeled into the lot. I took it as long as I could, and then, cursing, I climbed out of the truck, slammed the door so hard the whole cab shook on its frame, and went up the steps and into the bar.

The jukebox rattled. There was an odor of frying onions and hair spray. Behind the bar, the TV showed live footage of Delossantos's superyacht, pursued now by swooping helicopters and a flotilla of navy vessels. I found Rutherford perched on a barstool, in close conversation with a freakishly thin woman whose hair was dyed green and cut close to her scalp. She was gesturing violently, jerking her chin to emphasize whatever point she was making, and Rutherford, his eyes fixed on hers, just nodded and nodded again.

"Hey," I said, leaning in over Rutherford's shoulder, "remember me? A hundred and twenty bucks? Horton Hill Road?"

He shifted his eyes to me, flung-open eyes, dancing eyes, and grinned. "Oh, yeah, hey, I'm sorry, but Ginny"—he broke off to introduce her—"Ginny's having kind of a little crisis here and I just, well, forgive me..."

"My wife," I said, my voice stripped like a bare wire. "She's all alone, don't you get it? My wife? Remember?"

"Your wife?" Ginny said, raising her eyebrows. "You got a wife?" And without waiting for an answer, she said, "You don't look married to me." She jerked her head around and called out to the bartender, "Hey, Steve, this guy look married to you?"

"She broke her leg," I said, feeling it all come up in me. I was sorry for Melinda, for myself, for the world, so very sorry I was on the verge of tears. "And two ribs," I said. "And she's stuck out there with no heat and no electricity... Look, I just need to get home, okay?"

"My bad," Rutherford said. He pushed himself up, threw back his drink, and leaned in to give Ginny a flickering kiss. "Back in thirty," he said, crooning to her, and then we were out the door and crossing the lot and it was all I could do to keep from venting on him. The gravel crunched. The air was still and cold. We climbed into the truck, our doors slamming simultaneously, and then we were creeping back up the road, and the subject, the only subject now, was Ginny ("She's been put through hell, I mean, really—you have no idea").

It was past ten when we finally pulled into the drive, all my senses on alert, envisioning the worst, but then I noticed the soft, trembling glow of a candle burning in the kitchen window and beyond it another in the living room. Melinda was going to be furious, no doubt about it—*How could you abandon me like that?*—but I had the news on my lips, the catastrophe to seal the deal, and the phone, the phone too. I unclicked the seat belt and reached for the door handle, but before I could push the door open, Rutherford had hold of my arm. His face was a soft, swollen mass suspended in the glow of the dash lights. "That's a hundred twenty bucks," he said.

I counted out the bills, impatient now, but there was one thing more. "I've got to thank you," I said. "You're a lifesaver, really, but I wonder if you couldn't maybe come give me a ride into town in the morning? Just in case I can't get through to anybody, I mean…"

He didn't respond. The heater, set on low, breathed along with us.

"For another hundred and twenty, of course," I said.

"Ginny's the one with the troubles," he said finally. "And that's got to be my number one priority."

Melinda was right where I'd left her, on the couch. She was asleep, her breathing the only sound in all the dark vacancy of the house. I saw that she'd been able to get the sleeping bag out of the closet and arrange it over her legs, as well as managed to light the candles and bring a little cheer to the place. Which was good. A good sign. I debated whether to wake her or not, since the Olfputt was inoperable still and there was nothing we could do, at least not till tomorrow. I fingered the phone in my pocket. It still had a charge, but I'd shut it off to conserve the battery. Would it be dead in the morning? Of course it would. And then what? Then I'd start in all over again.

I decided to let her sleep. There was no reason to awaken her to the news of the world, the fingerprints of which were all over the place, as if it were a crime scene. The morning would be soon enough. But then the sleeping bag rustled and she sat up. "You're back," she said.

"Yes," I said.

"What happened? Did you go to the neighbors'?"

I nodded, though whether she could make out the gesture in the reduced light, I couldn't say. "We need better neighbors," I said.

"What is that supposed to mean?"

I shrugged, and let it drop. "No worries, we're going to be fine. You hungry?"

"I could eat. Those pills they gave me? They really knocked me out."

I thought of the steaks we'd defrosted in the meat compartment before the electricity went down, which wouldn't be good much longer. They could really have used a marinade or even a dry rub, but under the circumstances salt and pepper would have to do. Outside, it had begun to snow, a ghosting in the windows that was like static on a TV screen. Everything was silent. We were country people now and that was the long and short of it.

"I'm going to go out and fire up the grill," I said. "You want anything? A drink?"

She shook her head. She was tiny, shrunken, nested on the couch like some hibernating creature awakened before its time. "I don't want to risk it with the pills."

"Okay, that's probably smart," I said and poured myself a scotch before backing out the door with the platter of steaks and our only flashlight that seemed to be in working order.

I saw that the snow had begun to gather in wet clumps on the jatoba decking we'd selected for its durability and on the hood of the grill and the railings and the trees that snuggled in close to the house. I had no idea how much propane was left in the tank, but when I turned the knob and struck the match, there was a satisfying whoosh of ignition, and in the next moment the steaks were on the grill and I turned my face to the sky, where the tones shifted and coped and the stars hid themselves away.

I woke at first light. I could see the breath hanging in front of my face. We'd piled up all the blankets and comforters in the house, stripping the bed in the spare room and making do as best we could, but the fact remained that we were stranded and the house was colder than the interior of the refrigerator, in which everything was slowly going bad. I wanted coffee, but that was a luxury since all the water we had resided in two big pots on the kitchen counter, the pipes duly drained to prevent the further hassle of their bursting. In July. A new curse came to my lips, working itself around the four musical syllables of the name of the Earth's self-appointed savior, Delossantos.

It took me a moment to realize that Melinda was awake beside me on the fold-out couch, just lying there, stiff and silent, her rigid leg tenting the blankets. "I don't want to be helpless," she said. "I want to get up out of this couch and *deal* with things, okay?"

Whether this was an implied criticism or not, I didn't know, but I pushed myself up and slipped the phone out of the pocket of my blue jeans where they lay on the floor beside the couch. Predictably, it was dead, and here was the new reality. I was shivering, though I'd slept in my down vest, and I couldn't even start a fire, because we'd both agreed, in designing the house, that fireplaces were wasteful and just added to the burden of carbon dioxide in the atmosphere— they were an indulgence, and indulgences were what had crippled the environment in the first place.

Suddenly I was angry, furious. I took it out on the phone, flinging it across the room and into the waterless bathroom, where it clicked and hopped over the tiles before coming to rest against the porcelain wall of the tub. "I'm doing the best I can," I said, my voice on the verge of breaking, and then I pulled on my clothes, my boots, my parka and knit hat and went on out the door even as Melinda called, "Where are you going?"

I was greeted by the sharp rim shots of branches breaking under the weight of the snow that had accumulated overnight. There was a tree down across the back lawn and the Olfputt was nothing but a hummock in the snow—which was still coming down, everything suspended in a drifting haze. It was then that I detected movement out on the road we shared with the Zinssers, a car there, tires creeping, headlights fighting off the snowflakes, and I saw that it was them, our neighbors, in their gas-hog SUV, going somewhere because they could, because their car was operational and they occupied a house with an oil burner and water in the pipes and a fireplace and a generator I could hear blatting in the distance. "Hey!" I shouted, waving my arms, and then I was charging across the yard, desperate now, and if I ran right out in front of their car in a situation in which they'd be hard-pressed to stop, even with four-wheel drive, I was beyond caring.

There they were, two pinched faces caught behind the clapping wipers. The husband was driving—Art, Art Zinsser, the name coming to me suddenly—and I saw him wrestle the wheel as the front end skewed to the left and the tires caught and he came to a stop just in front of me, inches to spare. Snow settled on the hood, the exhaust coiled and fumed. What Delossantos hadn't figured on—or maybe he didn't give a damn one way or the other—was the formula, the recipe, getting the ingredients straight. How much sulfuric acid *do* you add to the atmosphere to get the desired effect? How much is too much? And how do you get it out?

Art Zinsser rolled down the window and stuck out his head. He was older than me by ten years at least, his eyes narrow and rheumy, his hair the color of talcum powder. "Are you out of your mind?" he demanded.

I put both hands on the hood to freeze the car right there. "We need help," I said.

Our neighbor listened without expression as I delineated the fine points of our situation, my voice clenched between my teeth, then dug in his pocket and handed me his cell phone, still warm from contact with his body. He didn't have a whole lot to say, and his wife might as well have been a mute, watching from behind the windshield and the clapping wipers, but I didn't need performative neighbors, didn't want gossip or the news or an exchange of recipes, just the use of his phone for a minute, that was all. I stood there in the falling snow till I got through to Triple A and arranged for the truck to come, then handed the phone back, thanking him elaborately, but he just nodded, no more eager for intercourse than we were, and what he thought of the Filipino billionaire or the shortcomings of EVs and self-designed homes designed without oil burners or gas-fired generators, I never discovered. I didn't find out where he was going, either, whether it was to buy out whatever might have remained on the shelves at the supermarket or just keep driving south till oranges decorated the trees and the sun began to do what was expected of it.

Overhead, the sky was as washed-out and uniform as the sky in a black-and-white film. I watched the Zinssers' car sculpt its way through the drifts and turn right at the intersection, toward town, then trudged back up to the house to deliver the news to Melinda. Soon, before the end of the day, anyway, we'd have a functioning car and beyond that a functioning house. Things weren't so bad, I told myself. It wasn't as if we'd depended on our garden for the essentials—it was supplemental, a hobby—and if the supermarkets ran out of things the way they had during the pandemic, there'd always be more. If they couldn't grow wheat in Kansas, they'd grow it in Argentina—science had gotten us into this fix and science would get us out of it. Things would be different, of course. Pricier. Less convenient. The trees would die. The squirrels would die. But the Zinssers and Rutherford and all the rest of them would go on living in their world and we'd live in ours.

A shiver ran through me. If anything, the snow was coming down harder now. I stood there a long moment, then turned round, went back up to the house, and got in under the blankets with my wife to wait things out.

A MACHINE IN
THE GARDEN

by JAMES KAELAN

THE GONZALEZES WERE THE first family on Dorchester Avenue to get a trailer. A white semi with an exempt California license plate idled down the street at half past seven that morning, eight days after the earthquake. And with a throng of people standing on the sidewalk, holding back their squirming children, the driver eased up the narrow driveway of the ruined house. Gloria Gonzalez, in plastic sandals and an old floral sundress, stood in the shade of a blooming jacaranda, reviewing a thick stack of papers with the city official. Fred, in jeans, a long-sleeved work shirt, and hiking boots, watched closely—a "There you go," a "That'll work"; not helping, exactly, but not in the way—as the three-man crew uncoupled the container, climbed back into the cab, and headed out toward Alhambra Boulevard. A boy on the curb motioned for the driver to blow the horn, and the driver obliged, rending the air with a deep, rumbling honk that seemed to shake the hot morning air.

After an hour and a half of reviewing the contract and releases—
Gloria wouldn't be rushed into signing anything—the official, sweat
gathering on his upper lip, opened the trailer and led the Gonzalezes
on a tour. The neighbors, watching from the yard, crept slowly forward, trying to get a glimpse inside. As they looked on, the roof-
mounted air-conditioning unit whirred to life. The power had been
out more than a week, and though a few folks on the block owned
generators, the sound of the cooling unit purring, without the accom-
paniment of a hacking gasoline engine, sounded bucolic—like a
mountain stream in spring.

The Thompsons, whose children had gone to elementary school with
the Gonzalez twins, were the first neighbors to enter the trailer. The
space, they discovered, was spare and modern—nothing at all like
the ranch houses and Spanish revivals on Dorchester Avenue.

"It was like being in IKEA," Craig Thompson said to his wife
after dinner that night as they shared a bottle of room-temperature
white wine under LED lamplight. In the crystalline glow, with her
brown blouse and brown hair and red lipstick, Craig thought Kalli
looked older and paler than she actually was—like someone who'd
been living for months in a bomb shelter.

"I thought it felt like a hospital," Kalli said. "You'd think that
Miguel and... I'm blanking on his name."

"Alexio."

"That they would've come back to help."

"I thought they were both stationed in Kuwait," said Craig. "Or
Qatar."

Kalli shrugged.

The Thompsons' daughter, Alyssa, had called every morning for
the first three days but couldn't get the time off work to fly home from

Atlanta. Andrew, six hours north in Sacramento, had sent a crying emoji on the family text thread and asked if his Ninja Turtle collection was safe.

Through the dining room window, Craig could see the trailer's roof, with its skin of blue-black solar panels, silhouetted against the permanent glow of the downtown skyline. He had been surprised to learn that the unit had a composting toilet that turned human waste into garden-ready fertilizer. The water filtration system made sink runoff safe to drink. But like everyone else in the neighborhood, Craig had been most curious—and, if he was honest, most apprehensive—about the printer.

The contraption was roughly the size of a large microwave, with a thick glass window that afforded a view of the lower third of the device's internal compartment. On top of the printer, like the display of an industrial copier, was a touch screen with four options: BREAKFAST, LUNCH, DINNER, and SNACKS/DESSERT. That afternoon Fred had pressed SNACKS/DESSERT, and then read aloud from the menu.

"Applesauce... chocolate chip cookies... tiramisu." He had a look of amused surprise on his face. "How can it make tiramisu?"

"One way to find out," said Craig.

"I don't think we should," said Kalli.

"What about applesauce?" proposed Gloria. "That seems nice and straightforward."

"Applesauce it is," said Fred, and pushed the button.

The machine began to whir. Fine gears in its core turned with a faint whine, and a nozzle lowered into view. After two quick calibrating jerks, the machine groaned, and the tip of the metal cone began to extrude, in slow concentric circles, a whitish-green paste made, apparently, from algae.

The Gonzalezes and the Thompsons peered into the chamber half-expectant, half-mortified, watching the gelatinous mound grow.

"Looks pretty delicious," Craig said, nudging Fred with his elbow.

"It looks horrifying," said Kalli.

After a minute and a half, the nozzle retracted, and a digital bell dinged. Fred opened the door, removed the tray containing the "applesauce," and set it on the counter.

"Who's hungry?" he asked sarcastically.

"I'll try it," said Gloria. She found a collection of stamped metal silverware and handed utensils all around—except to Kalli, who waved away the offer with a stiff outstretched arm and a shake of her head.

Gloria dipped her spoon in and tried a bite. "Well, it's a little chewy," she said. "But it tastes like applesauce. How about that?"

As the sun set their first evening in the trailer, Gloria felt nervous about turning on the lights. Showing off that they had electricity seemed insensitive. But Fred said she was being silly. "We lost our whole house," he reminded her. "The Thompsons didn't even lose a window."

Gloria also felt guilty about showering. She and Fred had been washing with the hose in their backyard behind a tarp they'd hung from the overgrown Chinese elm. Now, in the pristine trailer bathroom, the idea that you could summon hot water with just the turn of a valve seemed almost extravagant.

Later, while Fred washed up, Gloria inspected the kitchen more thoroughly. There was a dishwasher, but no garbage disposal. Beneath the sink were three bins: trash (the smallest), recycling, and compost (the largest). A two-burner induction stovetop sat beside the sink. And, of course, there was the printer.

On its left side was a removable plastic cover. Gloria opened the compartment and tried to inspect, without pulling it out, the cartridge of powder that, through some alchemy, became semi-recognizable food. She closed the lid and stared at the glowing display. Then she tapped DINNER and scrolled through the options, trying to imagine how each would print. Corn bread. That seemed plausible. But beef stew? Hamburger? Did the machine make the buns and the meat separately? Or, like the applesauce, was it just some blob that tasted roughly like beef and bread? And was the flavor from the algae itself? Or was there some other agent responsible for deceiving her taste buds?

She kept scrolling until she reached PIZZA. Gloria had rarely eaten pizza since getting embarrassingly gassy on a date with Fred in high school. But tonight it seemed, if not appetizing, at least intriguing. Why not? she thought, and pressed MAKE.

The printer purred, the nozzle lowered, made its jerky left-to-right calibration, and began to excrete a beige batter onto the metal pan in an expanding spiral. From core to perimeter, the dough turned golden, until, after four minutes, the machine had built up a par-baked golden disk ten inches in diameter and a quarter inch in height. Next, after a hiss and a beep, the cone began to secrete a red paste—tomato?—over the surface of the pie. After another readjust-ment, it discharged a white emulsion, not dissimilar to frosting, in a crisscross pattern over the sauce. Then the nozzle retracted, a venti-lation fan whooshed to life, and over the course of five minutes, the crust browned and the "cheese" melted into a semi-uniform sheet.

When Fred emerged from the shower, he and Gloria sat at the acrylic kitchen table, the pizza and two glasses of tap water between them. Gloria said a prayer. "Dear Lord, thank you for your mercy and your shelter. And thank you for this meal we're about to eat."

She paused.

"And for the machine that made it. Thank you for keeping us safe and strong through these challenging times. Even in our darkest hour, we see your mercy and your love everywhere. In Jesus's name, Amen."

"Amen," said Fred, winking at Gloria. "Let's eat."

*   *   *

That night in the trailer was the first time Gloria and Fred had slept inside in more than a week. Gloria had been standing in her kitchen, cutting open an avocado, when the quake began. She ran outside, still holding the knife, and stood on the concrete patio. The air was still, but the palm trees out on the street swayed like the Santa Anas were blowing. After a full minute of shaking, she watched through the glass panes of the French doors as the roof-mounted air conditioner fell in, smashed through the first-floor ceiling, and flattened the mahogany dining room table she'd inherited from her mother. Another minute later, as the tremor continued undiminished, the roof buckled and sucked down, the disjoined halves of the house toppling inward against each other with a thundering crash.

The old homes on the block, built in the 1920s and 1930s, had all survived. The ones that had collapsed—like the Gonzalezes'—were built by the McKendrick Development Company in the early 1980s. The machinations required to prove that McKendrick was responsible, if they even were responsible, seemed as complicated to Gloria as the internal workings of the printer. It did her no good to think about it.

The Thompsons, whose house was built in 1929 and had fared much better, had made up their spare bedroom for the Gonzalezes that first night. But Gloria couldn't sleep. She just stared at the ceiling, waiting for it to cave in. So, the next day, she and Fred dragged their mattress out of the rubble of their home, beat it clean, and slept in a ten-person tent lent to them by the Lius.

But then the heat wave hit. And Gloria, sweating through her nightgown, had tossed sleeplessly each of the six nights since, listening to the howls of the coyotes and the scurrying of the rats as they scratched through her ruined house.

Now, finally, lying in the trailer—on a memory foam mattress with the air conditioner cooling her face—felt like some uncanny dream of paradise. She was safe and comfortable, but just outside the door of this glimmering, futuristic box was the rubble of the house where she and Fred had raised their children. Gloria felt sick to her stomach. Then she felt a bubble of gas begin to worm its way through her intestines. When it came out, hot and hissing, it stank like rotting shellfish.

The day after the Gonzalezes' trailer was delivered, the Luongs received theirs. The following morning, the Sarkessians, the Emersons, and the Gomezes got theirs. And by the eleventh day after the quake, the final six homes on Dorchester Avenue that had been deemed unlivable had shelters in their yards. That afternoon, Mayor Valencia, accompanied by Luukas Pulkkinen of the Finnish firm that had designed the mobile homes, and Kenya Michaels, whose company had developed the printer, visited El Sereno.

By Gloria's count, nine news outlets turned up to cover the press conference. There were the local stations, but CNN and MSNBC had both sent trucks. And while a small stage was being erected in front of the Gonzalezes' home, journalists and their crews wandered up and down the devastated street, recording the wreckage, and asking people, if they didn't mind, to act out picking through the ruins for the camera.

Then, at 2:00 p.m., with a generator powering the PA system, a spokesperson introduced Mayor Valencia, and Mayor Valencia himself, who had just finished a tour of the Gonzalezes' temporary shelter, strode onto the collapsible stage. He wore a crisp blue long-sleeved chambray shirt and dark jeans, and the crowd gathered in the yard and on the sidewalks applauded him as he adjusted the microphone.

"Our city," he said, "has been hit by one of the largest earthquakes ever recorded on this continent. It was the Big One; and it got us on the chin. But we've been preparing for this."

Gloria found that she was having a hard time paying attention. The sun was beating down on the back of her neck, and her head was starting to ache from dehydration. Mayor Valencia said something that made Ben Luong raise his hand and wave, smiling, to the rest of the crowd. Then she noticed a number of people in the audience were staring at her and Fred with mawkish expressions. Fred smiled sheepishly. Gloria looked down at the ground, embarrassed.

After the speeches, with a gaggle of news crews following them, Kenya Michaels and her team from Foodtopia installed a phytoplankton propagation tank on the back of the Gonzalezes' unit. To grow the algae, Michaels explained, you needed a tank, salt water, a pump to circulate and oxygenate the water, and some live phytoplankton to seed the batch. "The pump runs off a small photocell," she said. "So, besides adding fertilizer once a month—which eventually will come from your own compost—you can generate enough calories for a family of four without doing much work or really spending any money."

Later, while the temporary stage was being disassembled, an anchor from NBC4 interviewed Kenya and Gloria together. "How does it feel to own a machine that makes free food?" the reporter asked.

"I don't think we own it," said Gloria.

"You do until you're back on your feet," said Kenya.

"That's very kind," said Gloria, her head throbbing. "But we really don't need it."

In their trailer that night, Gloria and Fred didn't turn the printer on. Instead, they ate peanut butter sandwiches. Gloria had recovered a jar earlier that week while combing through the remains of her kitchen. The bread, which was starting to harden, was a gift from the Luongs.

Next door, the Thompsons, still without power, ate canned chili by the glow of their battery-powered lamp. Through the bay window in their living room, they could see the Gonzalezes' trailer, bright with warm light.

"Can you even believe the handouts they're getting?" Kalli said.

Craig shook his head.

"The trailer is one thing," Kalli continued. "They need a place to stay. But this... printing your own food? And not having to buy anything... I'll be honest, it doesn't seem very fair."

"You grow tomatoes," Craig said.

"Yes, and it's a heck of lot of work. The tomatoes don't grow themselves."

"Maybe you should get some tomatoes that grow themselves, then." Craig winked.

"You don't think a machine that produces its own seaweed, and makes its own... its own..." Kalli trailed off. "I can understand during the earthquake. But when things go back to normal? What you eat... shouldn't you have to do something to earn it?" She stared at Craig. "Don't you think?"

"The earthquake wasn't even two weeks ago," said Craig.

"We'll see," Kalli said. "We'll see. Part of me feels like this has been the plan all along. Free houses, free food, free whatever, so you don't have to work anymore."

"But the Gonzalezes are retired," said Craig.

"This week it's earthquake victims, and next week it's Skid Row."

Gloria got up early the next morning and made a pot of coffee using a bag of freeze-dried grounds the Romeros had given them. As she had each morning since the quake, she took her mug and sat in the cactus garden, facing away from the vestiges of the house, until the sun climbed over the Chinese elm. In the last week she'd found her jewelry box, a coin collection that had belonged to Miguel, the crate of family photo albums, and the metal urn with her mother's ashes. She wanted desperately to piece everything back together. But the excavation was emotionally draining. She couldn't search for longer than fifteen minutes before she had to sit down in one of their metal patio chairs and cry.

Gloria could feel the sun cresting behind her, and so she started back toward the trailer. The new algae tank, more than eight feet long with a hinged lid, reminded her of a coffin. She walked over and swiped a window in the condensation that had gathered on the surface of the clear plastic cover. Peering into the tank, Gloria was shocked to see the black-and-white body of the Luongs' cat, Rinky, floating in the brackish water. She dropped her cup.

"Oh, sweet girl, no," she said, her voice catching. "How'd you get in there?"

Gloria went directly to the Luongs, still wearing her robe, and explained how she'd discovered the cat. Ben Luong—accompanied by his wife, Mei-Li, and their oldest son, Eric, who'd insisted on sleeping in his minivan in the driveway since his parents had refused to take refuge at his home in Diamond Bar—marched across the street to examine the tank. Ben had grown up on a farm in Taiwan and was not squeamish around dead animals. He reached into the green water and pulled Rinky out by the scruff of her neck. Hanging stiffly, with her front legs extended, she looked like a stuffed toy that had been left in the rain.

Fred figured Rinky had smelled the salt water, thought the tank was full of fish, and managed to climb inside.

"The lid of the tank weighs at least twenty pounds," Gloria said, exasperated.

"Cats are very clever," said Fred half-heartedly.

Ben Luong didn't suspect the Gonzalezes. It had briefly occurred to him that Gloria might have left the tank open and Rinky had somehow knocked it closed. But he felt Gloria would've confessed if she thought she was responsible. More likely, someone had coaxed Rinky with a handful of food and then deliberately drowned her. Perhaps it was even Craig Thompson. A few months back, Ben had seen him, in his Hawaiian shirt and navy blue shorts, chasing Rinky out of their front yard with a rake.

"They don't like our trailers," Ben said in his careful English. "Because they did not get what we have."

"I don't think anyone killed Rinky," Fred said. "I think she climbed in there on her own, and couldn't get out. And we just feel awful about it."

"Why does she climb in there?" Ben asked. "We feed her every day. Someone killed her. They want us to feel bad. And I know who did it."

"You don't," Mei-Li said in Chinese, putting her hand on Ben's forearm.

"Craig Thompson," Ben said, a hint of pride in his voice. "His wife made him do it—"

"I don't want to point fingers," Gloria said, cutting Ben off. "Let's all just try to forget about it."

Two days after Gloria found Rinky in the algae tank, just after night-fall, someone hurled a brick through the bathroom window of the Sarkessians' trailer. Ayda Sarkessian, who had just stepped into the shower, was so shocked by the noise that she slipped and cut her knee.

Saro Sarkessian, who at first thought the noise was a gunshot, immediately reported the attack to the police. They arrived three hours later. One of the responders, Officer Altuve, apologized for the delay. "There's been looting down in East LA," she said. "You guys are lucky over on this side of the ten."

"The other day, someone killed the Luongs' cat," Ayda said. "They drowned it in one of the tanks."

"The tanks?" Altuve asked.

"The algae tanks," Saro said, exasperated. "You think we are leeches? Come! Come to my trailer. Sit in my air-conditioning. Take a hot shower. Eat food from this machine. We will share everything we have. But no. They attack us, like we are thieves."

A week after their trailer was delivered, the Gonzalezes moved back into the ten-person tent they'd borrowed from the Lius. After Rinky was drowned, and after the Sarkessians had the brick thrown through their window, the Gomezes' container was tagged, in wobbly red letters, with the misspelled phrase THIS IS WHAT SOCALISM LOOKS LIKE.

That afternoon, Kalli Thompson came up the Gonzalezes' driveway carrying a plate of chocolate chip cookies. Fred, after spending two hours on the phone with the insurance company, had been separating what he had determined might be usable lumber from the rest of the debris, stacking it in piles according to length. He stopped and wiped the sweat from his forehead. Gloria, who'd been polishing a box of sterling silverware to keep her mind occupied, put down her rag.

"I saw you moved out of the trailer," Kalli said brightly. "I brought you cookies."

"How nice of you," Gloria said, her voice flat.

"They might not be as good as the ones your machine can print, but we like them."

"You really didn't have to do that," Fred said, coming up to take one.

"If you don't have plans tonight," Kalli said, "we'd love to have you over for dinner. The gas and the power are both back on."

Gloria made her best effort to shower behind the blue tarp Fred had strung up again from the Chinese elm. The water from the hose was painfully cold, even in the heat. She dried off, put on a green dress and her white sandals, applied a bit of makeup using her compact mirror, and walked next door with Fred.

As Kalli garnished the pot roast, Gloria sat at the dining room table with Fred and Craig, staring into the dusk light. She'd gazed out this particular window countless times in the thirty years she'd known the Thompsons. But the view this evening unsettled her deeply. Where her house should have been stood the abandoned trailer. Backlit by the setting sun, it looked like a black wall. She could make no more sense of the landscape than if she'd encountered it in a nightmare. *I dreamed the house was gone, Freddy. It was just so awful. Miguel and Alexio were stuck in Tehran and couldn't come home. They couldn't even call. Would you hold me until I fall asleep?* She had to look away.

"Do you mind if I close the blinds?" Gloria asked as Kalli entered the dining room with the platter. "It's hurting my eyes."

ON FORGIVENESS

by CAMONGHNE FELIX

WHEN MY MOM RETURNS from her trip through Germany, she returns with gifts.

For over a week, I'd meandered through life—my bath times, the walk to school—without the sweet, musky scent of her perfume following me. I had begun to grow resentful. Though I loved my grandmother and felt entirely safe under her care, I was young and old enough to feel threatened by the anxiety of object permanence, young and old enough to know that my mother might not return, young and old enough to understand that she might not have wanted to. By the fifth day of her trip, I had started to believe that I'd made her up. Things felt too normal without her, too predictable. Just as I would on any other day, I ate the same foods, walked the same route to school, watched the same shows at 3 p.m., whined for a Popsicle at 3:30 and got it. If she was real, why didn't her absence feel more disruptive? Why did I feel safe? How was I living without her?

I feigned illness during third period to call her, to hear her patiently stern voice tell me to go back to class, that there was nothing wrong with me, that she wouldn't be coming to get me from school, because she was about to go to class and would be busy for the rest of her day. I knew she would say this, and had grown accustomed to the disappointment I felt once she'd said it, but I called her anyway to nestle in the comfort of her voice, to be reminded that she was still there. I don't really remember having any childhood friends before sixth grade. I definitely had them, and I'm sure that my mother fed them my snacks when we played together after school. I know that I had birthday parties and attended birthday parties, but I only know this from the yellowing photographs that feature versions of my face, not from memory. I don't really remember much from that time except for my mother and me, hands gripped in the winter mess of a New York City blizzard, faces whipped in the wind, frostbite beginning to set in. We were cold and stranded by the late bus, no clue how we would make it home if it didn't show up. I was cold but I felt content standing beside her, in soft silence, content to die beside her if the bus never showed up and that was what was meant to be. I was her third leg, her pleasant burden. She could go nowhere, be no one, without me.

On the morning she returned from Germany, my cousins and I helped my grandmother clean the house. Ambitious, I chose the vacuum, nearly twice my size, pushing it with all my might, but still unable to meet the precision of my mother's vacuuming, which drew beautifully straight impressions into the brown carpet without effort. After what felt like hours of poor vacuuming, she walked through the front door, crossing the threshold in a puffer coat that dusted the floor. The house erupted into hugs and greetings, but I pushed past the cousins to get to her, throwing myself into her smell. "My baby!" she cried, and then I almost cried, but at the moment she embraced me and the tears began to feel like they might fall, I ejected myself from her grasp to look up at her, my rage coming forth like an opening.

"Aw, you're mad at me? Don't be mad!" she taunted, reaching back down to draw me into her once again, squeezing the quiet anger out of my little body.

"I brought you something," she said as she took her coat off and laid it across the arm of our small, low couch.

Sitting down, she pulled a brown bag out from the backpack that leaned against her leg. Out of the bag, she pulled a package wrapped in that tough plastic, the plastic you've got to cut with a knife to get it open.

"Look," she said, the plastic creaking and groaning as she attempted to free the object from its package.

"It's a magic toy! It says it's for little magicians"—I couldn't read it, because I couldn't read German—"and you can make potions with it. And then…," she said as she leaned in close, her voice a low whisper, her eyes glistening with mischief, "you can eat it!"

My cousins shrieked with disgust and delight. My mother and I stared into each other's eyes for a long second before I took the toy and ran to the corner on the other side of the room to begin my divinations. "Say thank you!" she called out after me, and I did.

It was not God who cursed Canaan, but Noah who cursed Ham.

I wanted to leave the synagogue out of this, but once I began writing, its absence felt unnatural. It was the second Black synagogue in Queens, New York, and we took two buses to get there every Saturday morning, since I turned eight. It was where we all met, in the pews toward the back of the sanctuary, where my soon-to-be stepfather would hover at the end of service to bat eyes at my mother. I barely noticed when it first began (I couldn't see much above his knees, because he was so tall) but I began to catch on when he came back to our section to greet my mother, then leaned down to thrust his cuff-linked wrists toward me, his fingers bonded tight to its palm, which held stickers he'd brought for me from his classroom. They were animal stickers, or maybe fruit stickers. I think I found them silly. I think I was entertained.

He was a rabbi at our synagogue, a young rabbi who'd only just graduated from rabbinical school and had the confidence of someone who knows they matter. He was a caramel-toned jock, gregarious and popular, and later I would recognize that he was quite handsome, at all stages of his life. Apparently, the matriarch of the synagogue had wanted him to marry her daughter, but my mother and I came along and, to her chagrin, ruined that plan.

I don't remember there being a date. I assume there is much I'll never know about the interiors of my mother's life, but I was attuned to the map of her movements, always clear on where she was, where she was coming from, and when she was expected to be home. What I remember is that some Saturday, late after service, we were in his secondhand Cadillac, hurtling down Farmers Boulevard toward the house we shared with my grandmother. I remember a dance, a dance in which my mother's medium waist glittered with thrill as he pulled her close. And then, I remember him eagle-legged on a dining chair in our living room, stuffing pill capsules with dry organic herbs, the dregs of it littered around his chair like catnip. He would let me help him sometimes, my little fingers a boon to the task.

We didn't say many words to each other, but we'd watch *Drop Dead Fred* and laugh together when Fred did something silly to Laura, forcing her to act out the drama of *his* imagination, making her seem like the unusual one. We would sit there for hours, stuffing capsules with his dietary materials, my grandmother isolating herself in the kitchen.

It was Noah who climbed from the ark with the impulse to plant a vineyard, the sweet grapes of pleasure a gift from God in return for his labor. It was Noah who drank the ferment, submitting to the original sin of gluttony, the moon whole and high and governing the night. It was Noah who had committed the fault of revealing himself in completeness to his son Ham after the moon had moved on and shuttled the sun into place. It was Ham who stumbled upon his father, asleep and still drunk with contentment, and it was Noah who had committed the fault of revealing himself in completeness to the world as he slept. And it was Ham whose restless open mouth— perhaps in casual jest, perhaps in alarm—revealed to his brothers that their father lay naked in the field among the vines. All knew of the truth, but it was Ham who had looked upon him first. His father had been revealed to him.

> And Ham, the father of Canaan, saw the nakedness
> of his father, and told his two brethren without. And
> Shem and Japheth took a garment, and laid it upon
> both their shoulders, and went backward, and covered
> the nakedness of their father; and their faces were
> backward, and they saw not their father's nakedness.

She came home, finally, and I went to sleep. I woke up months later, and she was pregnant.

The day was sopping with sweat. As usual, I was dressed in something that did not agree with the weather. Kit had not come to visit me, but to visit the cherry blossoms, which settle pink in the sun when they bloom. That was fine with me. I like pink. I liked Kit's gentle presence. I liked that she wanted to walk.

I was telling her about the night terrors I'd been having, about how every day the 4:30 a.m. hour became a witching hour in my body, about my mother, about the dark, about the industrial interior of some other world beckoning me, telling of war. I woke in a film of sweat, not sure which planet I was on or who I belonged to, having seen my mother's face on bodies I'd never recognize.

In one dream, my mother is a military commander of some sort, her entire body sheathed in the metal skin of armor. A pale dust surrounds us, the matte sky a blush-colored backdrop to the bareness of the planet. We don't speak but I can feel our connection like a tether attached at the waist. Suddenly she turns to me, and we are laughing together. My Earth body has no idea what we are laughing at, but the sound of the laughter itself is familiar, a note that marks the score of my childhood on Earth. Suddenly my younger sisters appear, and they are hungry. As I would in real life, I go to what looks like a refrigerator and pull random substances out of the canals of the cold box. I go to the counter to assemble the substances into something satisfying, or at least edible. I separate the mush into three bowls. There isn't enough. One of us will go hungry. The dream ended there and I woke up mortified, for reasons I can't explain, the heat of terror radiating from every part of my body.

Kit told me that I might have been seeing scenes from a past or future life, the images buried deep in a subconscious that has lived thousands of nonlinear years, a subconscious that has recorded hundreds of thousands of midnights come and gone.

"You really think our souls can hold on to all that evidence after we switch bodies?" I asked her, curiously defensive, wanting to poke holes.

"I work with this spiritualist who does past-life regression sessions," she said, ignoring my doubt. "She's Romanian or something and she has been a practicing spiritualist her entire life. I think you'd really get along. I'll give you her contact information and let her tell you about it. It's a thing, I swear."

"Have you done it?" I asked.

"Yes. You can go as far back as you want to go. I traveled through, like, six lives. And I learned that across all of my lives, I struggled to find purpose. So now I am going to focus this life on living purposefully."

We got lunch, talked about other things. All the while, my mind was focused on the dream state, 4 a.m. far away but approaching like a freight train. I could feel my mother's laugh on my conscience. I could feel her hunger. Before we went our separate ways, Kit urged me to make the call to her spiritualist. "I think she could really help you. I really do."

In the summer of 1999, my mother gave birth to a nine-pound baby. She delivered two weeks late. As a result, the baby was just *in* there, eating its own fluids, ingesting its own poop. I held this fact with a surprising amount of maturity, because I understood that humor dies with responsibility and now that I was going to be responsible for this baby, this human birth alien, I couldn't laugh at her condition.

She was an annoyingly quiet baby. I enjoyed the mischief in her cries, how it was a firepit, and how it drowned out the ambient city noise just outside our window. I couldn't believe that she slept so much. She had no hair. She had a little white crib, which we shoved into the corner of the bedroom all three of us slept in. I would sneak into the bedroom and pinch her with the edges of my fingernails to wake her up, just to hear the little sigh of her cry. I wanted to see her eyes.

As she began to become more and more of a person, I recognized her softness. I resented it immediately. I could tell she would be the kind of kid who would hang on to me, who would need me and love me despite my pokey little edges. She was there for the first hospitalization, and also the second. She was there for the first attempt, and the second. If you ask her, she felt nothing but the despair of pity. She was not angry at me, not even for sucking all the air out of the house as I fell further and further into illness, not even for having to witness me hurting myself, little patches bleeding through my yellow school uniform shirt. She says I was nice to her, that I protected her, loved her. I don't recall being nice to her, but I know I protected her. I tried to protect her from Mom. I tried to protect her from him.

He wasn't necessarily a bad father, just a self-interested one. I spent time with him that I remember with some limited fondness. I was like his child, he said, and I never doubted him, given the way he treated his other children. He embodied fugitivity, which normally I associate with liberation but in this case it was more of a limitation. He moved with abandon, his ethics colored by desire and impulse. If he wanted to take us out and relieve my mother, it actually meant that we would sit in the car under the tracks of the 2 train while he went on rapping with the incense man on the street. Some days we would sit for what felt like hours, the rainwater from the tracks falling onto the car's windshield in dirty splotches, my toddler sister next to me rambling about something or other.

About a year after my middle sister was born he just sort of disappeared, at least in memory. All I remember of him from that time was the nose-swelling scent of his whiskey, the scent of his Tiger Balm, the scent of his others. Each day was a slog, my mother attempting to start her career as an attorney with a nine-pound baby stuck to her body and an adolescent stuck to her leg. His neglect seemed so hateful at times, as if he didn't like her, couldn't stand to be around her. But then on a rare warm night they would disappear into the bedroom while my middle sister and I did whatever else, smiling like Cheshire cats as they left the small dwell of the bedroom. Time went by like this—spotty absences and colorful reappearances that never felt complete—and in sixth grade, she was pregnant again.

Once again, something inside of her was brewing. My mother's warm brown shade was darkening against the cold winds of an unexpected life. She was so tired, so, so tired. My stepfather had all this joy around him, it seemed. All these friends, all these places to go, people to see, Jon Jon and Jack and Yehuda. During an on-season they had conceived this tiny zygote, so small, even at eight months, that my mother seemed barely pregnant, just bloated, a little hard protrusion the only evidence of a human inside of a human.

Her pregnancy was easy this time, not like me, and not like the one that came before. It was not a welcomed pregnancy but a tolerable one, the one that would certainly be her last. Mom tied her tubes, said no to any more of a lifetime spent in the purgatory of motherhood, a space she did not like and never quite conformed to.

Right before the baby was born, he said he had to take a trip to see his father. He just *had* to do it, right then, one week before her due date. Mommy begged him, pleaded with him: "What am I going to do with these kids if you're not here when the baby comes?" He promised he would be back. He swore.

It was a Sunday. It was 2020. Her water broke. A neighbor called an ambulance. By the time the ambulance came, she was well into the throes of labor. They got to the hospital and never made it to a room. She gave birth in an elevator with no one standing beside her. He had not returned. His car had "broken down" somewhere on the way back. He was not back the day after my baby sister was born. He was not back the day after the day she was born. I went to school on Tuesday in my new pink Timberlands and *still* he had not returned. Mommy, little sister, the baby, and I all rode home from the hospital in a taxicab. The baby stayed awake and silent for the entire twenty-minute ride to our fifth-floor walk-up.

He finally appeared a few days later but I honestly don't remember it. By then he had become the single villain of our story. He had no point, no utility. He was useless.

It was then that something in my mother changed, and not for the better. Before work each morning she was blasting Mary J. Blige, crying as she wrapped her locks up in her head wraps, kissing our faces with dolorous joy, sucking up all the endorphins she could. She was a little gone all the time; unfocused when home, snappy, sometimes downright mean. But there was still a softness left in her, a malleability. She could still be his person if he wanted her. She continued to let him back in but with a bit more caution. She snapped at him when he snapped at me, which she had previously let slide, but it was like she could sense my endless opposition to him and for the first time could validate it, could understand.

When he lost her trial bag, her most prized possession, things began to change. For many attorneys, the trial bag is an object of achievement, even though it does nothing more than carry thick folders and legal papers. If they're an especially mobile attorney, they have wheels on their trial bag and they drag it around the courthouse like a bad child, shoving it through closing courtroom doors, and in between other bags in the elevator. That image is what my mother had worked for. It was what she had suffered for, what she had fallen asleep at the dinner table for, what she remembered and held on to when the six-year-old she couldn't find a sitter for spilled her dinner on the lecture-room floor when she was still studying for the state bar exam. This is the image of herself she held on to when she woke up at 5 a.m., pregnant as god knows what, to take that very exam. This is the image of herself that made her weep as we scanned *The New York Law Journal* and found her name among a list of tens of others in the tiniest print. He had lost the trial bag, thrown away that image of my mother that existed before him, that image that was the metaphor for all she was, and he had lost it so callously. "It was in my trunk and someone took it." Someone *took it*? We all knew this was a lie and he wasn't even good at telling it.

"Someone took it?" my mother raged. "No, you fucking lost my shit."

"Why did you leave it in there?" he retorted.

"Because I had no reason to believe it wouldn't be safe."

I think that my mom believed they would get back together. She kept making space for him, kept "when Abba comes back"–ing him, not ready to let go until she had to.

A couple months after his last disappearance, he reappeared at our apartment to pick my sisters up.

He had an important update.

He was getting married.

At the start of my past-life regression session, my hypnotist tells me to breathe, and to do whatever feels natural to me, to close my eyes, to put my head down, anything. We are speaking over Zoom, well into the pandemic, so she does not have the ability to hypnotize me in person, but it is not necessary, as I am somehow already bought in.

"If you can hear me…," she begins, her accent like honey, "I want you to tell yourself that your eyes are glued together and they won't reopen until the end of the session.

"They cannot open no matter how hard you try, because they are tightly and firmly stuck. They are simply, solidly, comfortably together. And let them take you in even deeper."

She continues, "Those eyes have relaxed. And let them take you in even deeper. I want you to first draw your attention into your eyelids and I want you to feel a very pleasant fluttering sensation right underneath your eyes. And when you feel that sensation I want you to nod your head."

A couple of seconds go by as I nod.

"Okay, great.

"And I want you to go ahead and take a deep breath in on the exalting feeling or emotion of gratitude. And say, 'I can remember and I can access a past-life experience. I come in with curiosity.'

"And, Camonghne, in this experience, if there's any heavy emotion, I want you to see it from up above like you're watching a movie. Whatever comes is fine, try not to think and analyze, just experience any image that comes up.

"Take a deep breath in and hold it at the top. On the exhale, release it into a deep state of calm. That's it. That's it. This state is very beneficial and healthy. That beautiful healing light, right above your head.

"Let this light be very strong and send it, right now, wherever your body needs it the most."

She pauses to give my brain time to work for my body.

"I am going to write down what you are seeing. I will ask you some questions to confirm what I see. When and if, and only when and if, I have the right answer, confirm by nodding.

"As I count from ten to zero, go so deep that your mind is no longer limited by barriers of time or space. So deep that you can remember experiences that you had even in this body or even in another body or even between physical bodies because you are far greater than this physical body. Ten. Nine. Eight. Seven. Six. Five. Four. Three. Two. One."

I was a small girl, no more than fourteen. Everything had a color. I had no nation, no safety, no name. I was alone, except for my grandmother, whose soft face and weathered skin comforted me. When I come home from school I slip out of my sandals, push the sky blue curtains aside, and crouch through the entrance to our home, calling out to the gentle woman who has become my caretaker since the death of my parents.

"Now think of an important milestone early, *early* on in that life, something that changed you."

I do not know why they died. I do not know when. It felt as if there had been some kind of accident. Perhaps I was too young to know.

"Your mother died."

My grandmother offers me a soft pastry, the edges round and crisp and cool with natural honey, the filling nutty and earthy. I have eaten this before. I know this mouthfeel, this texture, this taste.

"Okay. You are connected to her in this life."

Grandmother asks me about school. I tell her something nondescript, which indicates that school was likely uneventful. I played with my friends, I think. I practiced my letters, I think.

We were in an age when there was no television or moving images. And even if there had been, we would not have been able to afford any apparatus of the sort. I go into a corner of the large open space, each room separated according to its use with standing shades. Our home was decorated with soft pastels, wall-mounted fans. Everything pink and blue and purple up against the soft wood of the walls. Tucking myself behind one of the shades, I change out of my school uniform and into more freeing clothes, an old skirt and buttoned top likely sewn by myself or my sweet grandmother. I flip through a magazine for a while until Grandmother calls for me.

"Go back to another important event, later than the first. Maybe you're eight, or nine, or ten...?"

Grandmother asks me to run an errand. To go to the market for a small, necessary item. Perhaps a vegetable or a spice. Perhaps something as simple as salt. It is time to cook dinner.

"Are you in a big city, a small city? The United States?"

I set my satchel across my shoulder and let it settle on my waist, pulling my dark hair out from beneath the thin strap so I myself am not contained. I call out to Grandmother as I run out of our home, pushing the curtains aside once more to loft my way into the long and narrow street.

The streets are paved, so it can't have been that long ago. It may have been a before, or an after. In either case, I would not know where or why I was but simply that I most certainly was.

"Are you scared?"

I am bounding down the narrow streets. I feel nothing but the gentle elation of childhood, the happiness that comes with the freedom of a long walk, with the freedom of a single task, with the freedom of being young on a long walk with only a single task to complete.

There is a bend in the road and I fold into it, leaning left as my legs take me where I am meant to go. My perfect legs, which I trust to get me to the market and back.

It goes dark. Not completely, but dark as in how the dusk of night walks its way toward the end of day.

"Someone is following you. So what happens?

"Okay, I want you to know that you can actually watch your death just like you watch a movie on your screen and it's one hundred percent safe. Can you see yourself leaving your body until you are bodiless? You can go to that place after death."

A knife goes into my back and I plunge further into this unnamed darkness, hurtling toward a kind of eternal blackness that seems to overwhelm me. Before I fall down the shaft of death and completely out of view I turn back and see through a fish-eye the silhouette of a man. I never get to see him or his face very clearly but I can feel that he is looking plainly into mine.

Was it a young scorned lover who killed me? A violent stranger without impulse control? A hit man finishing off an old job? My own father, perhaps to cancel his progeny? My mother killing her child self?

"I want you to go into this universal consciousness, and tell me what you experience.

"You're still alive. You're dead.

"You're looking at yourself."

When Noah fell into the moat of his own pleasure, he had forgotten his own clothes. He had shed them in a sweaty haste and become belligerent. Noah was a joyfully indulgent man who had done the grand deed of saving the animals from the torrents of the Earth. This gave him the power of God upon Earth and God needs no self-accountability.

He had seen all he could see of himself and wanted to see it again, wanted to see each part of himself up close, like any one of us, and had fallen in over himself as any drunk one of us has done or might do and had not remembered to cover himself, had not remembered to hide, not when his naked self was so beautiful in its ugliness, ugly where it had grown rotten with dignity.

So when Ham came to see his father, he saw what his father had seen and they gazed at themselves together in this rare space of absolute presence, in the rare way that any child gets to see the true stuff of their father's inner selves, that rare moment when the parent exhibits a previously unsought humanity and becomes vulnerable in that new humanity.

Nearly a decade after he had run off for the chimes of greener grass, I confronted my stepfather at a Brooklyn Heights diner as he sat for lunch with my sisters, who had called me to come and meet them because they needed me. Straight from yoga in my stretchy vinyl leggings, my mat tucked up like a hoagie under my arm, I marched to the diner and sat with them.

I texted my then boyfriend, *I am going to see my stepfather. I feel like idk what's going to happen.*

It was cordial at first. He yelled my nickname at nearly the top of his lungs, overperforming his enthusiasm. I sat and picked fries off my siblings' plates. After some niceties, I got down to business.

"Can I talk to you privately? Maybe we can go to the back?"

I brought up my sisters' concerns. I asked him why he was being so unkind to my middle sister. I asked him why his wife was bullying them, saying awful things about me, telling my sisters that I would amount to nothing and that they shouldn't aspire to be anything like me. Why would he want to turn them against me? I had protected them. I had protected him. I had made sure they didn't see him, not as I saw him, and here he was working against me, like I didn't have the power to tug at the veil.

We exchanged some words. I threw a glass of water in his face. He pushed me off my chair. I ran outside and scratched his wife's car with my keys. He pushed me to the ground.

"I see who you are," I yelled at him as he attempted to shuttle my sisters into his car. "I know who you are and they might not see it, Mommy may not see it, but I do. And I will *never* forgive you."

I had always felt this disdain for him, even when I thought it was love. I made this vow on my mother's behalf (who would never see him, or admit that he had killed something in her), on my sisters' behalf (who can never see him the way I see him, because they are made from him), and on behalf of myself, a woman in a line of women who have given grace and forgiveness at their own expense, who have let the abuse and neglect by men they've loved be absolved and dissolved in the bloodlines of all the women who would come after.

He sped off into the busy Brooklyn road, and I knew then that in hating him, I had transcended him. I was free.

Only weeks after my hypnosis session ended, he fell sick. It was 2022; he was well into the sunset of his life, and had begun to lose lucidity. In his loss of memory and consciousness, he took to calling me. He called me often. I answered once, not recognizing the number, and hung up quickly, deciding never to answer again. He kept calling anyway, leaving lachrymose voicemails that lasted, at least, two minutes too long. "You know, you're like a daughter to me, man. And I'm sorry. I mean it. I wasn't always great but I took care of you. I tried my best. I hope you can forgive me."

It was not because of the way he treated me that I refused to forgive him. I refused to forgive him for the way he killed the version of my mother that most loved herself, how he sucked the life out of her, made her a mere avatar of the person who came back from Germany with magic in her pocket. I could never forgive the way he abandoned her, that gurney in the elevator, that cold taxi ride home. I chose not to forgive him, because of how he treated my little sister, my gentle little sister who received his dismissal and his neglect and his sadness.

Outside that diner in Brooklyn a decade ago, I told him that I saw who he was. That clarity had broken a cycle—a cycle of grief, a cycle of subjugation, a cycle of granting undeserved grace at the expense of the grace we need to give ourselves. He had cursed my mother, cursed my family, and I cursed him back.

He kept calling. I kept not answering. He kept leaving voice-mails. I deleted them all. I felt bad for him, and understood that he was feeling the imminence of mortality, and that he did not yet know if he was ready to leave his body.

And Noah was devastated by this vulnerability, dangerously devas-tated. He was frustrated that anyone but himself had come to see what he saw when he gazed into the river's shiny bath. In humilia-tion, Noah banished Ham's son Canaan and all Canaan's progeny to a life of slavery. Noah banished Canaan's son as penance for Ham's plainness of sight. Noah cursed them to hide his own uncovering, to hide his own carelessness.

It was not Ham or Canaan who had sinned, but Noah. And it was not God who cursed Canaan but Noah who had spoken with the power and authority of God to curse Ham and his children. With his tongue and no other power, Noah banished Canaan to a life as ugly as the sight Ham had seen.

In a past life or the lives that followed, does God require that Ham allow Noah forgiveness? Does God require that Canaan allow Noah forgiveness? Do Canaan's children owe Noah forgiveness because he is their grandfather? Does anyone? The Bible never says.

* * *

When he died, I cried as if to nurture my awful new freedom. I cried because he was dead, and because I felt sad for my sisters, and because I will always see him differently than they do, because I saw him as he was. I cried because even in death he was breaking their hearts. I prayed for his safe passage because no human deserves the idea of hell. And that was all the grace I had to give. I could not forgive him. I will not forgive him. And that makes me feel more free than if I had forced myself to try.

I know that he has shown up in past lives. But because I had finally learned the final lesson of our relationship, the nature of the curse that binds us in this life and all the others, he will not show up again in the future. In past lives I imagine that I tried to forgive him. I imagine that I tried not to see him, that I tried to pretend that he was better than who he was. But all I needed to heal was to accept that I had seen him, to accept that he will live in my memory this way, naked, cursing me with his ugliness, holding it against me.

There is no portal quite like a mirror. When I look at my sisters' faces I see the nakedness of a thieving man. When I look at my mother, I can see the imprint of him on her grief. She still blames the wife for his leaving. My sisters blame my mom for his never coming back. None of them have seen what I have seen. They will never see what I have seen, they will never gaze upon his nakedness, because he was my mother's lover and because he is my sisters' father and their gaze is clouded by a mirage of him. I saw him as he was, naked and cross with humiliation. I saw him clearly. My job was to remember the past in order to divine and shift the terms of the future.

At his Zoom funeral, hosted by friends in Ghana, my sisters' faces crowd beside mine, sullen with exhaustion and finality. It is still yesterday in the home of his origin and this is the end. I feel him waiting on me, asking my permission, asking for my grace. The rabbis will sit shibah. My sisters too.

Before the service ends, I muster up my final offering to him with an addendum: "May your memory be a blessing."

Life, in its hundreds of thousands of iterations, grants forgiveness. Children forgive. Gods forgive. I am neither.

lime dill halloween   by patrick keck

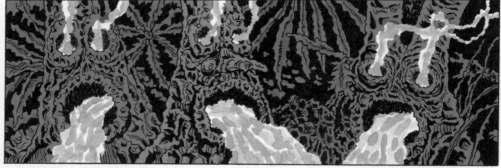

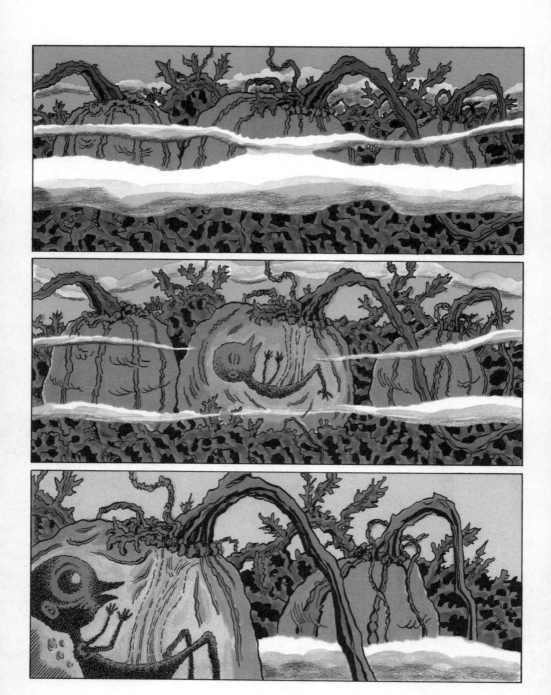

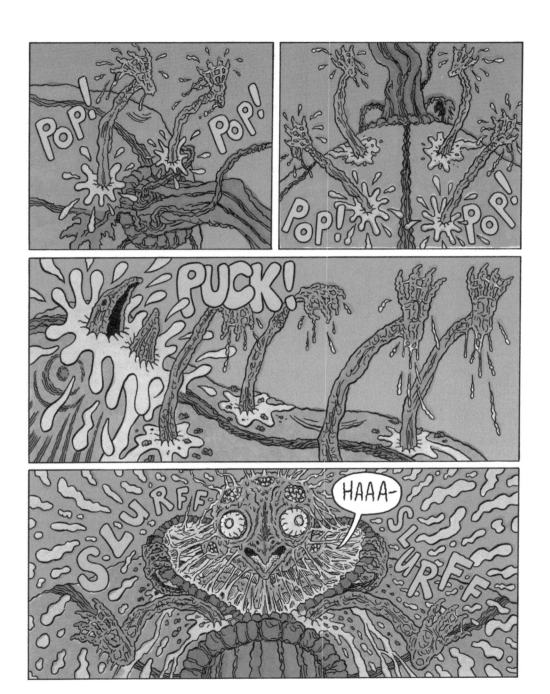

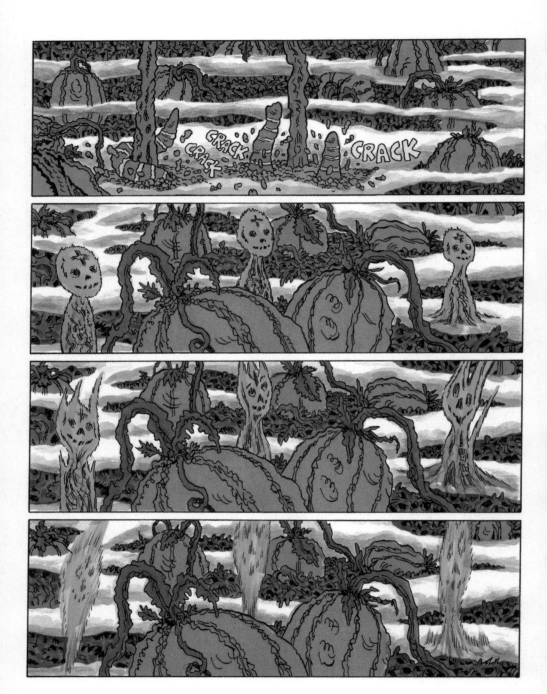

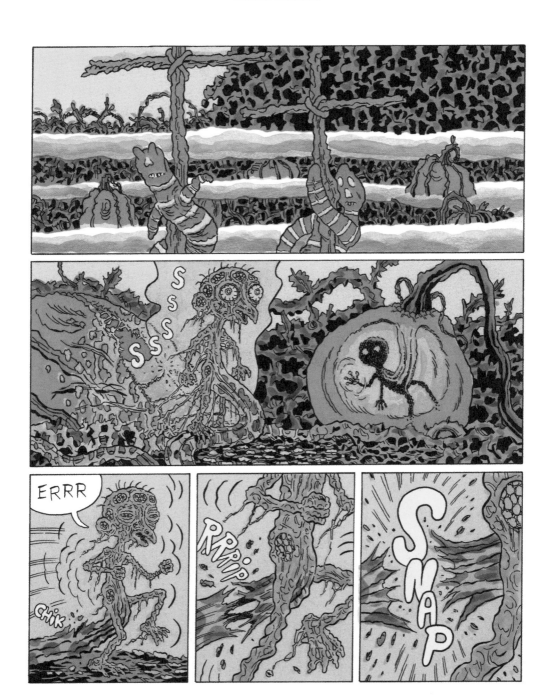

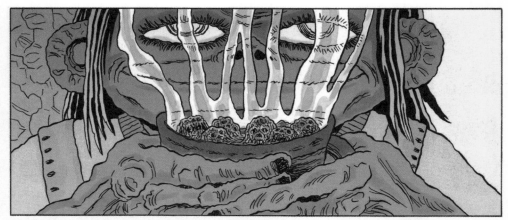

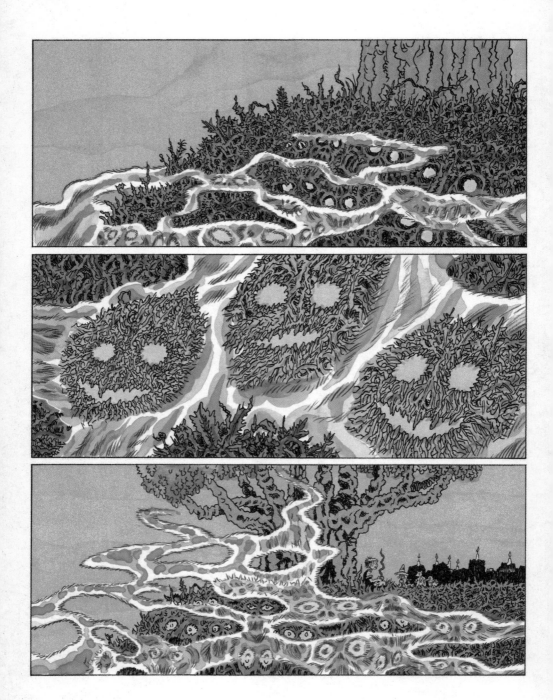

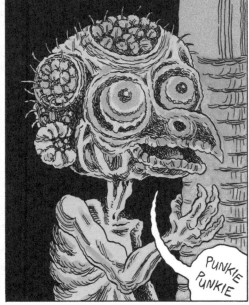

LOVE LANGUAGE

by CAROLINE BEIMFORD

MY HUSBAND WASN'T SECRETIVE about his private correspondence, but I didn't know anything about it until the pings from
his bedside table became incessant. *Say please and I might let u*, said
the message.

It has always been sweet but embarrassing that we have the same
passcode—the day we met—and I'd change mine if I could think of
a better one that I wouldn't forget.

A series of headless nudes had created the racket. The message
that preceded them was from my husband. *i'd kindly like to choke
you.* I scrolled a bit, then got the hang of the app and could see his
other threads, short, long, and with different moods and sensibili-
ties. I could appreciate that there was a skill to it, and saw that my
husband had little patience for slow or unimaginative replies. He
could not stay in the shower much longer, and I didn't enjoy being
a grubby little spy.

The cold cleared my head. At this hour, others on the street were equipped with dogs or officious fitness apparel. Slippers were bold for April in New England, but I would not be caught distraught over a few raunchy text messages. I dislike Boston. I make an exception for our block, which is leafy in spring and would soon be full of tiny wrought-iron beds bursting with tulips.

It felt dramatic to fly to Spain only a few hours later, but this is what I decided. The trip was planned, the flight already purchased, only I'd put it off weeks ago to recover from a cold. It warmed me now, to know I could reschedule.

I loitered in the street only as long as my husband would take to dress and prepare his small, strong coffee, surely perplexed by my sudden absence but preoccupied by the prospect of his teaching day. I waited an extra ten minutes in a muddy park to account for the commonest ways he made himself late: a stack of forgotten papers meant for students, the sudden desire, halfway down the block, for a handful of salted cashews, the dash back for a fresh shirt after taking the last step of the crumbling stoop wrong.

Our apartment was silent but smelled of arabica and shoe polish. The polish lingered from the night before, a weekly ritual. My muddy slippers I concealed beneath a scrim of summer shoes. I had ample time to pack and dress, but felt detached from these tasks and only in the airport looked down to notice the strangeness of my ensemble. A flimsy silk dress that would wrinkle on the plane and stockings with an uncomfortable waistband. Heeled clogs. Normally I wore thin, loose layers and comfortable boots.

* * *

The trip had never been urgent but I needed to use my sabbatical's travel stipend for something. Two weeks to visit the archive and see old friends. I haven't been back since meeting my husband at a conference five years ago. I lived in Madrid then. He lived in Boston. I agreed to move there after knowing him for only a weekend, which still feels bold, if not out of character. I'd been forty-two at the time, and knew the difference between whim and Providence.

When my friend Javi sent scans this March, the timing seemed perfect. My book was in a slump, it was still winter, and I had funding. What was a sabbatical for if not this? Now I feel like I am running. This is a comforting feeling, but in the way of falling back into an old habit—a Barajas cigarette, or a glass of aged rum before bed.

I can't stand hotels in cities where I've lived, and found an apartment on Calle de Juanelo a few blocks from the archive. Javi is busier than expected, and hasn't done what he promised. "What takes a day in Boston takes a week in Madrid," he says when I call. Three weeks, I think. What is he using, infrared?

"Will you have lunch with me?" I ask.

"I'm busy running the machine at lunch," he says. "For you!"

Javi still works at our old Jesuit archive and is meant to be using its new, refurbished CT-scanner to reconstruct the contents of water-logged ledgers dating back to the Inquisition. Old love notes passed between monks and disappeared as binding scrap? These are hardly the archive's priority. I do not adore my book's working title ("Intimate Cryptography: The Signs, Symbols, Locks, and Keys in Medieval and Early Modern Love Letters"), but the article did well, and the phrase "x-ray microtomography" seems to titillate even those committees that were once entirely against me.

Brother, the beauty of your spirit moves me in ways I have not experienced on this mortal plane. Speak to me. Look at me. I beg you.

"Not exactly fraternal," Javi had teased in his email nearly a month ago. "I can send the rest when we scan them. But maybe I won't, so you'll visit."

Now I am here, and there are no new notes yet, and Javi can't even take me to lunch. I pass the time by cleaning my rented apartment. A studio, and the landlord is selling it. In exchange for the amiable price, he has reserved the right to show it to prospective buyers at any moment, and the rooms must be immaculate when he does. The space is small. A kitchenette and bath tucked under a stair, which leads to a room that protrudes like a tooth from the gum of the canal-tiled roofline. The lofted space boasts a window in each wall and contains a low mattress, garment rack, and narrow folding table that serves for both work and meals. So far, the landlord has brought no buyers, but he arrives without calling to inspect the drains or glaze the sink.

After his chores, my landlord is prone to linger and I learn that his wife has died, and he is lonely and at loose ends. I know he lets himself in even when I am not at home, since I find evidence like his large, dirty footprints on the floors, which I keep meticulously clean. The building across the street is in the midst of being demolished, and a fine white dust covers the sidewalk and drifts in the windows. I cannot keep them closed. The air is too delicate, too soft and soaked in sun to deny it entry, though the nights are still bitter and the room does not trouble itself to retain heat. I sweep often, to honor our arrangement.

Last time my landlord appeared, he brought a cloudy, sweet liqueur that made my teeth ache when we drank it. He spoke of expecting the view from the apartment to improve considerably

once the demolition was complete, revealing the steeple of San Cay-
etano and the hill leading down to the plaza from two vantages. He
is optimistic these prospects will increase the appeal and value. *And
when a new structure is erected?* I wish to ask, though I decide not to
disturb his hopeful mindset.

Otherwise he speaks about his wife as though this is the thing
we have in common. Her nocturnal habits and wild temper. Her
unhappy Bilbao childhood. I am surprised to find I am interested in
his wife, and the way he speaks of her gives him a brooding, gallant
dignity he lacks on other topics. He dresses neatly in a narrow camel
coat and pointed shoes, as though his structured clothing seeks to
balance the roundness of the rest of him, of his head and eyes and
cheeks and gut. He is physically robust, though his spirit feels fragile.

I do not say much during these visits, three in the first two days
alone, and mainly listen and take tiny sips of my liqueur. At first
I worried about sitting back on the bed, and what it might suggest—
the table is equipped with only a single chair—but his mournful,
courtly manner puts me at ease. Normally, I would find his recur-
ring appearance a nuisance. Instead, his impersonal neediness is a
welcome distraction.

It has been three days since I left Boston and I have not called
my husband.

His alerts increased after the first night, and now chime frequently, far more than they normally do when I am away. I can't
tell what's come over me. He knows I've arrived and that I am safe.
I shared the details of my trip and departure with his department's
administrative secretary. He doesn't know where I'm staying, or why
I don't respond.

I don't know why myself. If I speak to him now, he will sense
I am upset, and I can't bear to admit it is over an app full of harmless messages. If I wait a little longer, he will be angry at the delay,

but I will be free to pretend that my feelings—disproportionate, possessive, mostly nonsensical, and sure to dissipate—never existed.

Dearest— begins the first of his texts. The word alone sends a pain to the base of my stomach, where I experience all strong emotions. I feel plagued by my dubious conviction that what is kept secret is always more true than what is freely expressed. I have not opened the thread since.

I go down to the archive to heckle Javi about the second note. Before we enter, Javi buys me a drink, though he spends the time complaining about his director and the other archivists, many of whom are sleeping with one another, or else trying to usurp his funding or seniority. Listening, I feel a blend of relief and fear, since this scene was once my own, and I haven't missed it. All of us over-qualified and striving, believing our little side projects would lift us out of the murk of our identical ambitions.

"Meanwhile," Javi moans, "I am getting less action than a pair of cloistered monks in the fifteenth century."

The ink contrast is low, and the images on the screen come into focus as though emerging from beneath lapping water. The notes, written on the back of scrap parchment from an earlier monastic man-uscript, have been sliced into strips and used to secure the newer book's pages between the glue of their endpapers and binding. Now that they have a micro-CT, the scanning itself takes little time, though Javi's system is slow with the programs that flatten the image, identify its layers, and rebuild the text from the iron and carbon in its ink.

As we wait and take turns at the monitor, Javi guesses there may be three or four more messages obscured within the scrap, all shellacked inside a series of mold-speckled spines from 1472. The monastery had a bindery at that time, and Javi guesses either the writer or the recipient of the notes must have worked there. If the second book contained the fragments of a second note, what was to stop the third, fourth, and fifth volumes from containing them as well? In the recent scanning of historical manuscripts, it isn't uncommon to find notable fragments, but in the realm of lost letters? A series is rare. We are both giddy but Javi lets me take over the controls. He is quicker with Old Castilian and Latin script, but I am better with the software and have more experience manipulating 3-D images. My own setup lets me target specific metal salts for better dating, but at the moment, all I want are the words.

At last, the voice emerges.

Bright face, dear one, what outcome do you seek from withdrawing yourself from me, as a stag eludes the hunter? You hide within these walls and rooms, yet these halls we must share forever. Stop this. I hunt not to harm or trap you, but to taste again that nectar of love and friendship so sweet to me and new. I would lick it from each finger were I given leave to feast from you once more. Though let it not be once only. Let us play again, brother, as He cannot but bless. (And how can He but bless that which is so sweet?)

I could have waited for the scans to arrive in my email in Boston, if Javi ever got around to making them, but this, *this* is what I came for. The shock of a voice recovered.

Necromantic is what our work can feel like some days. But once a voice is raised I am easily mesmerized.

Bright face, dear one.

i'd kindly like to choke you.

I can't remember all the messages in my husband's private correspondence, but certain lines had a grim charisma.

On the weekend, Javi and I are invited to dinner at the home of old mutual friends, a couple with children now who have moved outside the city. Javi offered to host us in Chueca, but his bachelor's garret has a bathroom with no door, and the couple doesn't like to bring their children there. I was disappointed not to enjoy the view from his large terraza, but the couple said even this was spoiled, since it sits above a famous bear bar, and the noise from the street is often raucous.

For his part, Javi dislikes visiting the couple all the way in Las Rozas, since he claims they don't use enough salt, and nothing they serve has any flavor. We decide to meet and take the train to Las Rozas together. During the trip I decide I have no choice but to confide in Javi about my situation.

"Our marriage is very free," I tell him, by way of context. No children. Few constraints. "It's a marriage of spirit," I find myself saying.

"Uh-huh." Javi nods but I suppose I may sound insipid to him: he has never believed in the pacts that people enter when they are in love, least of all those that govern their future selves. "So then what happened?"

I describe the anonymous messaging platform and how I encountered it, but remain at a loss for how to characterize my reaction.

"That's it?" Javi asks. "No meet-ups?" Not as far as I could tell, I say, though meet-ups were not out of bounds. "What did he say when you asked him?"

"Nothing," I tell my friend. "I came here instead."

"I don't understand."

"There's nothing to confront," I explain. "Only we still haven't spoken. It's been nearly a week and I can't seem to do it."

Javi's glee has abated. He used to glory in the dissolution of my relationships, but now he appears concerned.

Javi has never met my husband and only ever called him "el príncipe azul," since within weeks and months of meeting him I had abandoned my life in Madrid, moved into his university-subsidized Back Bay brownstone, and been plucked from the obscurity of church-funded record restoration to be delivered onto the American tenure track. To dismiss Javi's teasing, I describe for him the ways we are well suited and alike. Both Americans, though prior to Boston we seldom lived there. Both academics, mostly nomadic, though his recent work with electrons in ancient minerals has made everyone want to keep or woo him. Never married, if often paired, and both relieved, well into our forties, to have dodged the standard attachments. Neither of us had ever been the jealous one; always the one to stray. We hadn't expected to be pierced with this sudden and intense connection, and we were honoring it, but in our own way.

"Okay, okay, but what does that *mean*," says Javi. "Do you sleep with other people or not?"

"We can," I say. "We have."

"Huh," says Javi. "But no nudes."

"This is what I mean. My feelings don't make sense."

"Is it because they were hidden?" Javi suggests.

"We have the same passcode," I tell him, hoping he will bring some fresh perspective. "We don't message this way ourselves, since we're mostly together."

"I can't tell if you're jealous," Javi muses. "Or repelled."

i don't share pics of this cock with just anyone. prove you can take it.

i'd kindly like to choke you.

use your words. these balls won't suck themselves.

We are interrupted by the train reaching its destination, and once we've changed to the next line, Javi becomes busy telling a story about a person he knows with a secret life—a secret child and secret real estate—which he seems to think is topical, though the story has nothing in common with my own predicament. Javi irks me with his lack of insight and I interrupt him.

"It's not the situation," I tell my friend. "It's my *reaction*."

Javi appraises me with a squinting look that I know will precede a patronizing comment. "This nonrestrictive clause you've got. How often do you use it?"

"Not so often," I respond.

"What about him?"

"I don't really know."

"If you had to guess."

"I'd be surprised if it was more than the times I'm aware of," I find myself answering. "And they didn't bother me."

My friend looks unconvinced. "It's very stylish now not to be bothered."

"We aren't being *stylish*," I tell him. "I can't tell you what a relief it's been to know I won't ruin things simply by being myself."

Javi nods but continues to squint at me as we sway and lurch with the braking train.

I am saved from further questioning when we arrive at the house of our friends, a brick semidetached townhome in a row of townhomes all needlessly cramped beside a sprawl of scrubby field and a lonely traffic circle. We speak mainly of their youngest daughter, who they fear is being bullied at school on account of her mixed-race heritage and strange name (the name is strange not for reasons of heritage, but of parental taste). They have recently purchased a Secret Keeper on the advice of a children's psychologist and have urged their child to confide in the doll about all her troubles and worries. Confession alone has been shown to help in mild cases, but in the event that concerns escalate, there is also a website and manufacturer's code that will let parents access the recordings. For an extra fee, they can enable Active Listening, and get alerts at each utterance of a flagged phrase.

At strategic intervals, Javi orchestrates a diversion, and both of us use it to sprinkle the salt he has hidden in his pocket over the food.

* * *

The next day, my landlord arrives to repair a crack in the plaster. He lingers after, and I offer him a drink. I purchased some rum, to side-step his offer of liqueur. I recline on my bed and ask why he is selling the place, when he seems so attached to it. The apartment was his wife's art studio, he replies, and important to her. "She used to come here to paint and get away from me," my landlord admits. "I wasn't supposed to bother her, but I'd get impatient and come anyway. She'd pretend I was a buyer and seduce me." My landlord smiles. "'How much will you pay?' she'd say. 'How much? How much?'"

When he is finished remembering, I beckon him to join me on the low mattress and he eagerly accepts, shucking his coat and pointed shoes before climbing closer. I take pity on him. Seven months he's been alone, he says, though for me, it's been only seven nights. My landlord has a shiny, large head and hairy body, a kind face, shy hands, and a grateful, tortured muteness that radiates from him even in the midst of passion.

My husband is more leisurely, playful, dominant, and less hirsute. He pinches and hums, impersonates the provost, and laughs when he comes like I have told a surprising joke. I cannot help but think of my husband's petitions. *Use your words, old man.* "Speak," I order my landlord. He grunts without pausing. His eyes remain tightly shut. With more delicacy, I try again. "Tell me what you're thinking."

Eyes still closed, bobbing above, he shakes his head politely. "I'd prefer not to."

"I won't mind. Whatever it is, I'd like to hear it."

My landlord groans and ruts, then looses an anguished gasp as though I've wrenched it free against his will. "I wish you were her," he moans. "I wish you were my wife."

* * *

When he leaves, I experience the stomachache I have been feeling lately. It was no great surprise that the man was thinking of his wife. It is far more unusual for me to think of my husband. In the past, each little intrigue got its own separate lane. Not as a rule, but as a reflex. Missing him this way feels humiliating, like a final defeat after a long standoff. I consider opening the messages on my phone but feel this would only exacerbate the problem.

Javi has messaged about another note, which I can come by to read tomorrow. I want to respond that I ever so stylishly fucked my landlord and it hasn't solved anything, but typing it out, I see it sounds childish and delete it.

Out my window, the gutted building is a shadow between its neighbors. On the left and right, the windows are lit, and those left unshuttered reveal their occupants. A child at a table frowning at a workbook. A man removing his socks. In my favorite, a couple gropes each other on a too-short sofa, their feet splaying high into the air like a dolphin's tail. I don't think they are so young, though they have a youthful, teenage vigor, and it is only their bare bluish bulb that taints the scene.

In Boston, walking along our street, I can always tell from a great distance when my husband is at home and waiting for me. Our lamplight is the most golden of all the windows in our building. The wreck across the way is not just a shadow but a grid of shadows. The glassless holes where windows once were are even darker than the dark facade.

My husband's messages arrive in pings and little buzzes very late, and continue through the early Spanish morning. I could silence them, but what would be the point? Madrid is loud and I have grown unaccustomed to it. Boston is barely a city when it comes to sound. So sleepy and intent on minding its own business. On Calle de Juanelo, no one seems to bother with murmuring—passersby bark into cell phones or else hoot and call out among their groups.

Voices, motorbikes, music all clatter over the cobbles and up the crevasse of the narrow street.

The hubbub of my old neighborhood is familiar and dear, but I sleep poorly. I hear each time a patron enters or exits the place on the corner that opens at four in the morning. There was a time I went there often for the music, but I can't help balking at the thought now. My husband still likes to stay up, stay out if the occasion presents itself, and is able to forge a conspiring pact with whoever surrounds him. Though he's always a baby in the morning. Demanding toast and orange juice squeezed fresh. Eventually, the pings subside.

I know I have by now become the bad actor, though it is no longer a role I relish. I thought with my husband that I was safe from this impulse, but it is as though my instincts have reawakened and grown craftier. A last gasp of self-defense, Javi might speculate, against the life we were bricking up around us. But I had abandoned Javi's camp five years ago, and his suspicion of anything like dependence makes him the wrong voice to hold in my head.

All my problems, at present, are problems of correspondence. The world conspires this way.

I cannot express the measure of my joy that you are well. I have said you cannot hide your face from me, but to think of it blazing with fever or white with death is much bitterer. Some may have seen me and thought me too much concerned with your welfare, but surely you will not blame me for feelings you have caused. Still, you will not look to give me comfort. Nor address me with honeyed speech. You have found another companion. Is it true? The very one I have praised for his care of you.

We peer at the monitor in Javi's office, which smells of his oily breakfast cake. "Monastic breakups must have been hell," he says. "What a way to destroy all evidence."

"Or preserve it," I suggest.

Javi looks skeptical. "Not even the Renaissance foresaw micro-CT."

"I know it's greedy," I admit. "But I wish we could read the responses."

"Are you sure there were any?" Javi stuffs his mouth with the last of the cake. "Seems like we're witnessing a massive blow-off."

"Lovers' quarrel," I say.

"Look who's talking."

It has been eight days since I have heard my husband's voice. Low, resonant, and a little plummy. *tell me about your mouth.* Since the conference, drifting from the height of a minor podium, I have never gone so long without it. Had he mentioned the app before? It was entirely possible.

Dear one, now dear to another, you split my soul as a tree struck in a storm. I hate the one you look upon now, one who I know looks upon you with equal sweetness. I have seen it. Yet I am not granted even my hate, bright face, for how can I hate that which you so cherish? He who, graced by His will, could cure you when my own prayers did nothing.... You leave me riven with such thoughts as should not inhabit one breast. I have lost your love and friendship, yet do not wish you pain, when that wish would be a mercy to me, as it would mean I no longer loved.

The speed at which the letters are revealed has increased. I suspect Javi wants to be rid of me, or at least this version of me. He has his own life and problems and I'm surely proving needier than he'd expected.

"You *lured* me here," I accuse him, when he asks about my flight.

"Silence is the worst of all possible punishments," Javi states. "It's beneath you."

He is right, but I resent it. "You never used to side with the men."

*   *   *

Javi has begun to give me pitying looks when I show up at the archive, desperate for another note or companion for coffee. I re-read the letters, wait for the next one, then return to my apartment, dreading my landlord's appearance, though I only ever find his foot-prints and all the lights on. The money I left to stay the second week was returned in its envelope. ("How much will you pay? How much? How much?") I feel chastened by the monk's devotion. My own so easily threatened and full of vanity. I have never needed a body's every whim, but the rest? I feel stingy, grubby, small, and faithless.

In the morning, Javi emails about a final missive, incomplete but mostly legible, and presumably the end of our trove. "It's bleak," reads his message. "But at least we know how it ends."

...I ask only your mercy and grace. Look upon me, dear one, bright face, not with that special sweetness, but as a rich man gives alms to the poor. Cast at my feet that which is plentiful to you and so precious to me. A look, a smile. I will say no more to you of sweetness and honeysuckle, nor the torch of your soul.

My phone sits in my pocket, dead from neglect. I walk home quickly, uphill. Across the street, they've smashed through most of the facade and upper floors, but have halted after some unruly portion of the exterior crashed into the street. Now there seems to be a problem with the machinery, and the wrecking ball looms but will not swing, menacing the surrounding structures even in stillness.

From my apartment I can see the flocked, sun-streaked wallpaper in one of the rooms, and the stained interior of a low tub in another. Indecent, to leave the building this way, like it has been bombed.

A built-in china cabinet, perfectly intact, sits flush with the rim of the wreckage, its porcelain knobs painted pink with red rosettes. Our knobs at home were gifts, bronze and oblong, and cast from the pits of stone fruits by a friend with a forge in the suburbs.

My charging cord is short, and I find myself crouched on the cold floor, peering at the dark object with an intensity that borders on panic. Two minutes, three. After four, the screen alights. *Bright face.*

Dearest—
No goodbye?

I scroll past my husband's innocent early inquiries.

I've spoken to Marina at the college. I'm relieved but
confused. Why reschedule so abruptly?

Has something happened?

What's wrong with your phone?

I know you're safe. Marina guaranteed it. I hope you know
this won't tide me over long.

The messages fret and scold before darkening by the third day.

Have you met someone? Won't you even call to tell me?
What have I done to make you treat me this way? 3 days, V.
Where are you?

Really? Nothing? I can't stand not knowing what's
happened or even where you're staying. You wouldn't need to

*tell me if you'd just write back. I'd make that trade. Your
response for an explanation.*

*Call, send any word at all and I won't demand a single
answer. I know you're there, and working, but what else?
I want to know and don't.*

*I take it back. I want to know. I always do, but enjoy that
you return to me freely, that nothing else matters or stays.
Tempering, you called it once.*

*Is five years so little time that you'd go without a word?
Disappear as though you'd never been here, leaving nothing?
Your dirty hairbrush, a hundred shoes—everything is left
but you've poisoned it.*

*I hate speaking this way. Know you'll laugh at these poor,
pathetic messages on a screen. What do you want from me?
What have I done? I want to unsend every text and make
you feel as I am feeling. Like one of the poor souls you entice
and then ignore. Have I been demoted without a sign? Just
days ago I would've sworn we had never been closer. A fool's
thought, apparently. Pride before a fall.*

*Am I meant to come to you? Is this a test I am failing or
passing? And when will I know?*

*I thought perhaps a fling. You'd indulge and then resurface.
I was trying to honor our pact. I'm coming now. A response
might stop me, if you're reading this. I'm not sure what's
worse. That you read and feel so cold toward me that you
show no impulse to ease my suffering. Yes, suffering. Or that*

*nothing has reached you, that you haven't wanted to know
what I might be feeling. I can't remember our last conversation. You gave me no warning it would be our last. A
cruelty, if you knew. When you were never cruel.*

*I'm coming to find you. If only to make you tell me what's
happened.*

*No? Nothing? I'll wait a little longer. I feel I don't know
you at all right now, yet still can guess what you'd prefer.*

I am scouring our life for reasons.

*There hasn't been anyone since you left—if you care to know, if
it's relevant to your calculus. It feels disgusting to me to be with
someone else if you've left me. Isn't that funny? I feel like an
animal. A beast from myth and legend. You've made me this
way. Even if we are done, can I ask for a single night? So I know
that the last is happening. So I can despoil you into remembering
what you leave behind. Fuck some sense into you. Let me try.*

*I was drunk, but won't apologize. Come back for the sake of
my liver alone. Pick an organ.*

You're missing the tulips.
They're already budding.

I call my husband quickly. I haven't thought about what hour it
is there or what I'll say. We were serious after only a weekend, why
wouldn't a week suggest an ending? I'd been complaining about
Boston, and being a spousal hire. I'd groused for years about the
weather and the restaurants.

I hear when he picks up but doesn't answer. Instead he breathes deeply down the line. Heavily, like he's run for the phone.

I want to throw myself at his feet now and also make demands. *All your correspondence*, I'd say. *To me. To me.*

THREE STORIES

by DIANE WILLIAMS

EVEN BEFORE
YOU SPEAK

"Let me tell you," her father liked to say, "why I think I am right, and you are wrong even before you speak."

That was that memory.

It was against this background, to a large extent, that she thought of something else from the past—and before long, she was sitting in a boat with the wind hitting the side of the boat—watching the creamy highlights on the water.

She was thinking pleasant thoughts, and she chugged along, although the wind was against her when it was time to turn around.

It took forever for her to sail home, and when she arrived, she was scolded by her father.

Her father, he is, of course, the last and greatest father she will ever have.

She married and had three young sons, whom she frequently hears playing outside—their high screams and also their lower tones, or harsh barking. Could be dogs.

She supposes that she is of such higher rank.

SOMEONE
ELSE'S STORY

THE GROCER, WHOM SHE counted on, he said he was reaching out—asking customers what they really wanted—and then she saw fresh kale for the first time!—ruffled as it is—in a big bunch, and such a severe, deep green, more like something lavish she would prefer to wear.

She doesn't buy or cook kale, but it's as if she attacks the food that she does buy and cook.

And she can eat it very fast, impaling items that then hurtle into the pit.

Look here—she and her husband must hurry—they have urgent business to take care of just like everybody else.

Her legs serve her well as levers. They bear her weight.

And her husband, Jimmy—oh, just sum it up!

He is a new man these days, because he is different and she is new too—because they are both old now, and they walk more awkwardly, but can still go forward as they please.

How did this woman meet Jimmy? His dog approached and she petted his dog in, say, Paris.

Then their romance—and how they loved it!

Such times can be piled high and arranged like flavored ice cream in a fancy dish, and these were.

There followed a marriage and decisive difficulties. Still, she thinks on some occasions, she is safe.

So, now, setting aside all other business, the woman pulls a blouse on over her head, tucks it in a little on both sides and at the bottom.

The item is in the style of the period, and good-looking enough, although the fabric is guaranteed to fray, stain, or shrink.

It had been given to her by a friend who said, "Do you like it? Or might somebody you know like it? I've never worn it."

Want it? The garment? She has it on.

Topping the garment is her whole head, there in the mirror.

Certainly her head is not anything she wants to wear.

VERY WELL

NOBODY IS HELPED BY this, but he felt that his panic was necessary.

"Glad you came," Cassandra said.

He found a private place to take cover from the crowd in her... in the oblong bedroom, before he left her house quickly.

How often in the past, in that room, he had drawn Cassandra toward him, twisted her about, pressed her, stretched her, and bent her.

Was that only to his will? Apparently, because he now understood that she was finished with him.

Plenty of other things continued to go wrong—including the loss of his honor and the news of a dear one's death.

His fridge in the morning—his sink and his little stove were submissive enough, and he told himself—I always just put this in, when this does that!—a drop of olive oil into the oatmeal when he saw that the cereal seethed.

There was no requirement he knew for his gruel to foam or to go overboard.

On his early errand out to get the paper—why was he thinking this simple outing might be frightening?

He turned up then what he'd never known he had—a tiny, grooved shell in the pocket of his coat (no solid lump)—and in the other pocket—a piece of a shell—veined, and slick as if lacquered— nearly a dugout canoe shape that his forefinger slid easily into.

Just long enough, he was clutching at nothing much.

THE CASE OF
THE MISSING LIVER

by AHMED NAJI

Translated from the Arabic by Elisabeth Jaquette

I.

I SAW THE NEWS on my timeline. Practically all the rappers, groupies, and backup singers, as well as a few people working in the scene, were posting their condolences for the late star: their friend, their brother, and so on, and so on. Daddy was dead.

It had been a short-lived friendship. That's what I thought as the news sank in. But then it hit me that I'd actually known Daddy for seven years, no short space of time.

I loved his voice, and was crazy about his energy onstage at street parties or fancy hotel weddings. Suddenly I felt overwhelmed by time, the way it crashes down on us in numbers and news articles. So I decided to go to the funeral, maybe to bid goodbye to time itself. I don't know, these existential thoughts and emotional tangents make me paranoid and keep me from thinking straight, so I prefer to act without thinking too much.

The reason I'm saying all this is to explain how I found out about his mutilated body and missing liver. Maybe I'd hoped that intriguing little detail would make my own life more interesting, by flaunting an array of mangled body parts the way a peacock flashes its feathers.

I called a friend of the deceased who lived in the neighborhood, to find out where the funeral was being held. Fifty picked up the second time I rang. He told me that he'd been detained for questioning and was just leaving the station, but that he'd try to make it to the funeral.

Things were out of place.

But police were on the case.

2.

I was the arts reporter for a women's magazine, and I wrote a feature or two each month. I kept asking to do a story on something that, at the time, I called "street music." Street music, mahraganat, electro-shaabi: whatever you called it, the music was fast-paced, high-energy, and insanely popular. And after I had been insisting for ages, my editor finally gave in. But from then on, my editor told me exactly what she thought, especially whenever I filed a story and attached a few poorly lit photos I'd taken with my phone, none bigger than two megabytes. "No, Ahmed, no... This isn't the kind of work I expect. I can't publish any of it—look, they're doing drugs in this one."

My editor was waiting for a piece about some band, a bunch of college kids who sang in foreign cultural centers and postured as singers from the street. Instead, I turned in blurry pictures of teenagers from Salam City in their flashy clothes, masquerading as gangsters on streets flooded with wastewater, while hazy in the background were the rapidly built slums that had popped up after the earthquake in the '90s.

As for drugs, there were two pictures of Daddy holding a blunt, its embers glowing like a miniature sun. In the photograph he was a skinny fifteen-year-old, hadn't even started shaving. That's how fans would remember him: in his golden era, before his life was cut short.

The first time Daddy and I met was over in Figo's cramped shop, to do an interview for an article that never went to press. I kept addressing him as Mohamed Abdel Salam, his given name, but everyone else just called him Daddy. His coarse, kinky hair was grown out, with relaxer combed into it, and slicked back with shiny, greasy gel. I figured the nickname "Daddy" was some derivation of Abdel or Abdo, but being a journalist I feigned ignorance and didn't venture a guess. When later that day I asked, "Why do they call you Daddy?," he sang a snippet of a song I'd later hear him perform in concert many times. "Quit messing around. / You're with Daddy now." Then he stopped singing and said plainly: "Stick with Daddy."

Anyway, the article didn't get published. And even though Daddy never asked me about it, I'd occasionally sense a bit of a smug look in his eyes, like the time we were in a studio session with Figo, and later Haha, too, and he sang the lines: "A friendship I regret today. / He marked my heart, he cast his shade. / He made my smile fade away."

Two years after we met, Daddy would appear on television for the first time, and I would be the one who got him there. Everyone in the neighborhood would watch the broadcast and let out a celebratory trill when Daddy appeared. His rates for weddings would go up, and then—watch out, world!

3.

Fifty hadn't exaggerated. The government was there even in death.

I didn't meet up with Fifty on the day of the funeral, because there was no funeral service on the day I planned to see him. Forensics collected the body and examined it, issued a report two days later, and then turned the body over to his family for burial. The service was held that evening, after his family laid his mangled body to rest.

At first, I thought Fifty was exaggerating when he told me about the mutilated corpse and missing liver. But the violent nature of his lifestyle made me think it was perfectly reasonable that Daddy—who often sang about violence, weapons, thugs, brawls, how to oil your knife and clean your enemies' blood from its blade—spent the last minutes of his life in a fight. The basic details I overheard at the funeral that night all lined up. Daddy was found dead in his small ground-floor flat. His body was cut to pieces, and his liver was gone.

4.

I continued to follow the story, and as more details came to light over the next few days, an idea kept popping into my head. Finally, I rang Fifty and asked him to meet, but he said he was exhausted from being called in and questioned again and again. He didn't have time. I didn't pressure him for an interview. I was more interested in finding out exactly which part of the legal system was pursuing the case, and which prosecutor was doing the interrogating.

I asked two colleagues from the magazine's crime desk for help digging up more information, but they told me everyone involved was staying tight-lipped, and that signs indicated that authorities were on the verge of identifying and apprehending the killer.

5.

I met with Ali, a.k.a. "Ducky," on my way to Salam City to see Daddy's home for myself. For years Ducky had been my way into the world of mahraganat music.

My world was about as far as it gets from Salam City and El Matareyya. I grew up middle-class, with no great ambition to change the world and plenty of prejudice about all the things I knew nothing about; I was completely uninterested in anything beyond my social class.

Ducky was a skinny brown kid who exuded sex appeal in everything he did, all the way down to how his sweat smelled when he danced. Or at least that was the case when we'd first met more than ten years earlier, when I was introduced to him as a contemporary dancer at the Rawabet Theater. I don't know how he got from Salam City to downtown, or how he discovered the world of contemporary dance, but he was a member of a troupe that rehearsed in an old garage-turned-theater. The space and the troupe both received generous funding from the European Union, to support cultural dialogue and uphold Europe's reputation as a patron of the arts: typical soft power.

Ducky had clearly proved his skills in winning Europeans' trust and money. When I met up with him downtown all those years later, he'd put on a little weight, wore flashy clothes and glasses with yellow frames, and his long hair fell to his shoulders. He looked more like a pansy from Zamalek. Too upscale. He traveled and performed with local and international dance groups and participated in all sorts of performances and festivals. He'd also received a grant to dance in France, and had taken advantage of the opportunity to learn the language. He could speak it fluently now, and even though his reading and writing were weak, when he returned he made a name for himself as a choreographer and spread a rumor that he had a diploma in choreography. He also slept with a certain Frenchman—a cultural relations official—and so his little dance troupe consistently received generous funding from the French.

We shook hands on the corner of Mahmoud Bassiouni and Champollion Streets. We chatted a little, and then I told him I was on my way to Salam City to pay a visit to the Abdel Salam family. I hadn't gotten a chance to give my condolences to Daddy's mother, who missed the funeral because she'd still been in the hospital. Ducky said he'd come with me; he'd heard the police had found the killer. It was probably just another victim, though, some poor schmuck sacrificed to put an end to the media circus around the whole thing.

We decided to go together and took a bus with air-conditioning out to Ain Shams. We sat next to each other, behind a huge woman who looked like the epitome of Egyptian motherhood, aside from her long ears: they stuck right through her hijab and resembled those of a donkey, except they weren't covered in hair, just skin the same color as her complexion. As a result of spoiled food, carcinogenic pesticides that have infiltrated most of Egypt's soil, and high rates of pollution that multiplied with radiation leaks and the use of coal to generate power, a whole new landscape of illnesses and genetic transformations has emerged. And just as Egyptians have adapted to their environments and rulers for thousands of years, they were also able to live comfortably with all this.

I found out that the last time Ducky had seen Daddy was about a year ago in Marseille, when he was singing in a festival under the banner of "miraculous revolutions" and the Arab Spring. Ducky may have had a polished appearance and a veneer of class, but he still stopped mid-sentence and hocked, gathering the saliva in his mouth, then spitting it onto the floor of the air-conditioned bus. I concealed my disgust, and focused on whatever he was blathering on about: his project choreographing a dance performance based on mahraganat songs, and the theme he'd picked out, the rise and fall of Daddy, a local mahraganat singer who'd made it to the world stage.

Ducky had been hoping to get Daddy's approval to use a song in the performance, but now that he was dead, he was probably trying to solidify his relationship with Daddy's family to get their permission.

It took only half an hour together for me to remember why I'd stopped hanging around with Ducky: he was completely uninteresting. Back then, I'd put up with him because he was funny, but as he'd grown older his sense of humor had given way to a weighty French artistic solemnity. When we first met, his smile was stuck to his face like a contact lens on an eyeball, and he used his sharp wit to bridge the class gap between his world and that of downtown, with its dancers who often greeted one another in English. We used to sit in coffee shops late into the night, smoking shisha cut with a bit of hash, and two or three times I hung out with him at his home in Salam City. It was on one of those occasions that I was introduced to Daddy, who was just fourteen at the time. His dancing was a mix of hip-hop steps and Michael Jackson moves, and sometimes he performed with a group hired by weddings to fire up the party. He and his friends would go to the wedding, get onstage behind the singer, start dancing, and throw the groom into the air. They earned fifty pounds a gig, and a catered dinner too.

6.

Ducky and I arrived at Daddy's family's home, a small flat amid apartment blocks that the state had quickly constructed to shelter victims of the earthquake in the '90s. His mother welcomed us in, hugged Ducky, and shook my hand as we both murmured words of grief. Her face was pale and her eyes red but she seemed to be holding it together. She had two daughters and Daddy: her youngest child and the only boy. A photograph of him was hanging in the living room; in it he had short hair and smiling white teeth. The picture was an old one, a photo of a mother's son before he became Daddy, and a black sash hung across the frame. A recording of the Kuwaiti imam Mishary Rashid reciting the Quran emanated from the speakers in Daddy's room, which I remembered visiting years earlier. This had been his headquarters, where he met with people, recorded, worked, and had fun, before he was able to rent a little shop on the ground floor. Later he connected the shop to a flat with a bedroom and a living room, and that became his artistic residence, covered in color, graffiti, cables, speakers, recording equipment, hard drives, and CDs.

We sat with heads bowed while the recording played of Mishary Rashid reciting the Quran, in accordance with the rules of how it should be pronounced and avoiding any blasphemous melodies. He spoke so quickly that there wasn't even a second of silence for us to contemplate the verses or engage in a moment of sympathy. We sat there quietly anyway, and before Ducky or I could say a word Daddy's mother burst into tears. A man in a gray galabeyya sitting next to her tried to soothe her, murmuring, "There is no god but God, there is no god but God, Sister," and I guessed that he was Daddy's uncle. His mother wailed louder, and the grieving uncle looked like he was losing control of the situation. A boy of about twelve scurried toward him and handed him a bottle of water, and then the uncle gestured at us to enter Daddy's bedroom. A woman emerged from the bathroom, smoothing the black abaya that cleaved to her corpulent body, and she proceeded to hug Daddy's mother, who practically disappeared as though swallowed by a great black whale. Finally, we pressed on into Daddy's room with the boy, who headed to the computer and turned the volume down slightly on Mishary.

7.

The mahraganat star's bedroom contained a double bed with a stiff and tattered cotton mattress, a two-door wardrobe, and a sofa with a wooden frame and firm cotton pillows covered in fabric with a large floral print. The third wall was occupied by a table with a computer and sound recording equipment. This equipment was what Daddy started singing and recording on before he met the Doctor; before the cash flowed in and he opened the shop as the headquarters for his gang, his "team," as he called them in English.

8.

The last time Ducky had been here was with me and a French journalist. She'd paid him fifty bucks to show her around Salam City and meet Daddy, whose star had begun to rise. He'd also told her that he could translate for her, but instead of actually doing it he took me along and then tossed me in to interpret when she interviewed Daddy. I didn't realize that she'd paid him fifty dollars until Fifty told me.

We'd sat in the room and Fifty had been there, too, observing. He didn't interrupt the conversation, but he also wouldn't stop playing with his long tail right in front of her. At this point, I should mention that Fifty was a werewolf. When he was young he'd been bitten by a salawa, a doglike beast that some people thought was just a myth, but as is usual in this country, what people dismissed as mere legend soon manifested as a waking nightmare. They took him to the hospital and gave him a rabies vaccine, but the active ingredient was contaminated so it only half worked, and as a result he half transformed. He had the legs and tail of a wolf, thick, soft fur covering his back, and, according to some, the ability to smell betrayal. He'd smelled it that day in Daddy's bedroom with Ducky and the French journalist. "There's something fishy about that kid," he said after they left.

"I know, man," said Daddy, reading the look in his eyes. "I know."

9.

We left Daddy's building after sitting with his uncle in silence for several minutes. I hadn't said more than a sentence of condolence to his mother when we came in, and didn't dare ask his uncle how the investigation was going, not in the middle of Mishary Rashid's recitation and with Daddy's mother's wailing. Ducky invited me to hang out with him in his brother's pigeon hutch on the roof that evening, but I couldn't stand any more of his boring company, so I made an excuse and went for a walk instead. The sidewalks of Salam City were covered with puddles of wastewater. Little islands of algae bloomed on the surface and long grasses grew around the edges, effectively transforming the area into an urban green space, and improving the air quality to boot.

That night I walked toward the shop, the place I'd often met up with Daddy over the years, and also the scene of the crime. When I arrived, I found the door cracked and a red light shining from inside. I pushed the door open and Fifty appeared. The shop had been turned upside down, the bathroom tap was on, and water was overflowing onto the black ceramic floor tiles. Fifty had rolled up his trousers and was bailing water out of the shop. We didn't hug or shake hands. Several chairs were piled on the desk, and I lifted one off, adjusted it, and sat down. Fifty had lost a lot of weight. I took a piece of hash from my wallet and started crumbling it into some tobacco against my palm.

Fifty said the government had caught the killer, a kid named Steel, who had gotten into a fight with Daddy at a wedding a few days earlier. Ten days after the incident he turned himself in and said he was the one who'd killed Daddy, but the liver still hadn't turned up. The kid had apparently thrown it away.

What with the whole liver business, the government suspected Fifty, but to be honest they were always suspicious of the local were-wolves, jackals, and fox pups. Those three sections of society were known for their love of human liver. But they found the last call Daddy made to Steel on his phone, and when they pulled up the recording it was clear that plenty of insults were exchanged, each of them threatening to fuck the other's mother or sister. I interrupted Fifty mid-flow. "And where were you that night?"

10.

"My Lord most merciful of souls, which our eyes have longed to see $$ Oh Lord forget their savagery $$ And be pleased with them $$ Oh Lord terrible is the torment of the grave, turn their graves into a garden of the gardens of Paradise."

These were the words I found posted as an update on Daddy's personal account, there in front of me. I messaged him right away. *You ok man?*

A reply came in less than a minute: *May Mohamed Abdel Salam rest in peace, this is his nephew, we're opening his account for prayers and excerpts from the Quran. Mercy and light on his soul.*

I shifted in my seat in front of the computer. I wrote to the account of mercy and light, asking which of Daddy's nephews he was. I knew Khaled, who was closer to Daddy and sometimes hung out with us, but it was Hamza who was operating the account. I'd seen him bring food for the family when I was there with Ducky, but hadn't really met him, given everything else that was going on.

I called Khaled and asked him how he was doing, and he said he was still sad about his uncle, but he'd started thinking about singing himself and wanted to go to weddings, so I invented a white lie and said I was doing a story about Daddy's family. I told them I wanted to meet him and Hamza in their uncle's room, to photograph them and talk to them. Khaled got excited; his uncle had often introduced me as the media guy who had gotten Daddy on television.

The rest wasn't hard. Hamza had access to Daddy's Facebook account from his tablet, and from him I got the password. Actually,

I logged on to Daddy's account from the tablet and changed the password. I also went through the rest of his stuff in the room while I was chatting with the boys.

11.

I had wanted to sift through Daddy's archived messages when I got home, but I couldn't, because my girlfriend was in a bad mood. She had decided to come over for some comforting, and so the evening was lost to laughter, moaning, and her sweet company.

After she left the next morning, the first thing I did was enter the new password to Daddy's Facebook account. I spent time reading his messages and archives, and sipping green tea—this was my attempt to start the day with a healthy diet, an intention that I renewed each morning and abandoned by evening with consistency. I looked in his inbox and pulled up his messages with Fifty. The last one was sent about two days before Daddy was killed. And I can say with confidence that the motives for the crime were all there, though there was no actual evidence of Fifty's involvement in the murder of his friend, brother, and companion.

Very few people might understand what their last conversations meant. But I, by chance, was one of those few: I'd been there for plenty of the details they discussed in those final chats.

12.

From a production standpoint, the process of recording, mixing, and distributing mahraganat songs went against all market norms. First, mahraganat singers didn't exactly recognize intellectual property laws, and lots of them borrowed phrases or even whole songs from one another. They uploaded them online and made them downloadable by anybody for free, and so the songs spread from tuk-tuks to mobile phones to computers in net cafés and pool halls.

As the West, and particularly France, grew more interested in mahraganat music, Ismail, a.k.a. "Cabbage," appeared, a graduate of the German school and a failed rebel against social hierarchies. For years he'd tried to blaze a trail into the music world, only to spend years playing metal songs with English lyrics at small, cramped, and sporadic concerts. Cabbage was getting older, and when his father passed away, he used the money he inherited to open a small studio, which he turned into a production company called Dawayer Studio.

Ismail had picked up his nickname during the years he'd spent playing heavy metal. I didn't know where the name Cabbage came from, but Daddy teased him about it behind his back, saying he refused to eat grape leaves and always chose the stuffed cabbage instead.

Ismail descended on Daddy and the mahraganat boys like a paratrooper, by virtue of his facility for more than one European language. He marketed them abroad, provided them with high-tech recording equipment, sold the boys' songs to YouTube and other platforms, signed all the contracts, and gave them a few thousand pounds in return.

In the mahraganat world, the only contract that counts is your word. And Cabbage's words were just lies.

Two years later they found out that Cabbage had been introducing himself as their business manager and taking a cut of their profits without telling them. Meanwhile, Daddy's group had expanded to include Doctor Haha, Fifty, Ghost, and various other friends, fans, and followers.

Daddy stopped working with Cabbage, but less than a year later, the Voice of Egypt company appeared on the scene with the aim of monopolizing all the artists, by bullet or bribe. Daddy refused to join and decided he would rather go back to his roots: recording freely, uploading songs himself, and relying for income on concerts and weddings. But the messages in front of me made it clear that Fifty wasn't happy. They revealed that Fifty had actually signed with Voice of Egypt. But at the time, he was still in Daddy's shadow. Fifty was the echo of Daddy's voice, the hype man when Daddy sang. I could see in the messages that the Voice of Egypt company wanted to buy the rights to all the songs that Fifty and Daddy had collaborated on, and Daddy had refused to sign, and at this point their disagreement had escalated from arguments to threats. So how had all this sat with Fifty?

"You're killing me, bro," he wrote in one of their conversations. "You're stealing years of work that belong to me."

I was no criminal investigator, but I knew I'd discovered something in all these messages and threats from Fifty. It was clear that Daddy had responded to them by trying to contain the situation, and he'd refused to sign or work with Voice of Egypt. "Because they're a military company, and if you hand yourself over to them today, they'll have their foot on your neck tomorrow." I picked up the phone and called Fifty, who surprised me with a big hello and an invitation to his engagement party.

13.

Life had calmed down.

I arrived at the compound gate and mentioned the name Fifty, but none of the security officers seemed to recognize it. "You here for the party, sir?" one of them asked. I nodded. He looked at my ID card, wrote down the information, and pointed me in the right direction.

I arrived at the villa and tried to take in everything around me, registering that all this was an engagement party *for Fifty*: mahraganat star and Wolf of the Mic. No street, no stage, no weed to smoke, and no lights—instead there was a sprawling villa garden with a DJ at one end, a swimming pool, and guests everywhere. The villa was a white three-story building with green windows and doors, and walls engraved with the wings of birds of prey. In front of the main villa was another building, modern but smaller: a one-story pool house.

I didn't see anyone I knew, though there were several film and TV stars I recognized, people who worked in entertainment and advertising, the owners of fast-food chains. Not a whiff of Salam City's wastewater.

I spotted Doctor Haha in the corner. He was standing with a spliff in his hand, smoking serenely, by himself as usual. I started walking over to him, but halfway across the yard I felt a length of fur wrap around my right arm and grab me. It was Fifty's tail.

"Dude…"

His face split into a wide grin. I shook his hand enthusiastically, and to my surprise he hugged me with exaggerated gusto. Before we could say hello I heard a strange panting sound and someone calling his name. He apologized with a laugh. "Guys, come here and I'll introduce you." He took me by the hand and I saw that his fiancée, whom he'd apparently started calling "guys," was Fatima, a well-known actress, comedian, and singer.

Fatima had appeared on the scene a few years earlier. She'd started off as a comedy actress, and since she was skinny, with prominent bones, most of her roles relied on her body as the butt of the jokes. Then she decided to change all that, and underwent a series of cosmetic surgeries. At the time, the trendiest procedure used blubber extracted from seals instead of silicone, but for some reason the operation ended up resulting in a genetic shift. After her mutation, the public started calling her "Seal Face." Her features became more feminine and she even developed a wattle, like a turkey's. Her voice changed, too, and she gained new singing abilities that actually helped advance her career. She earned critical acclaim alongside opera stars and singers from the Gulf, and now she was on her way to marrying Fifty, a rising mahraganat star more than twenty years her junior.

14.

They turned up the music after midnight, and from inside the little pool house you could see the whole garden without hearing a thing, probably because of the acoustic insulation and double-paned glass. I liked watching everyone move to the music in apparent silence, save for a gurgle of water coming from the en suite bathroom.

Then the sound of the water ceased, and I heard the click of high heels on ceramic tile. A woman's voice interrupted my reverie as I gazed at the silent dance scene.

"Bulletproof, soundproof, heatproof too."

In the room was a wide bed, and two massage chairs you could connect to an app on your phone to control how they massaged the muscles of your legs, back, and even your ass. Across from the chairs was a glass table and a plush sofa, and sitting there was Doctor Haha. There were lines of white powder on the glass table in front of him, but he preferred the lit joint in one hand and the can of beer in the other. In the corner in front of him was a plain-looking desk, and behind that sat Mr. Barakat, dressed in a suit that was too big for him—as it had been since he first laid eyes on it, and as it would be when they buried him in it.

Doctor Fayza Nahawy extended her hand in greeting. I shook her damp palm, not knowing why I was here or who Doctor Fayza was, aside from having seen her name listed as managing director on TV networks like Hayat, Al Tahrir, and Tanweer. I also knew that she was a partner at the biggest advertising agency in the Middle East, one with a monopoly on news sites and online ads. She launched into a long speech about technology, the internet, a new world, a market filled with opportunities, and—most of all—YouTube (which wanted to steal our hard work, suck up our energy, and spit us out without a cent), but I didn't understand what she was getting at. She kept on talking, while I nodded and smiled, and when she stopped for a moment to catch her breath between sentences, I looked at Doctor Haha as if to say, *Come on, man, what does this have to do with us?*

Doctor Haha passed me the half-finished joint, and Doctor Fayza seemed to take the gesture as a sign that I was getting restless. She went over to the massage chair and sat down, then took out her iPhone and kept talking.

"Look here, Ahmed, here's the deal: What I want from you is a written, methodical work plan. How we can rein in those kids on the internet and save Egyptian music."

Silence filled the room. She picked up her iPhone, typed something on the screen, and then turned to Haha.

"I mean, can you tell me why there's not a single nationalist mahraganat song, not one about the army? Why is that? We want people to love you, we want your songs on TV, and we want you making money. Why not?"

After my third hit on the joint, my nerves calmed down and my muscles relaxed. I looked at Doctor Fayza. "All right."

15.

I'd never had more than twelve thousand Egyptian pounds in my bank account in my whole life, but after one month of light work, meetings, and planning with Doctor Fayza, my bank statement showed fifty thousand. All in just a month. It reminded me of a line in a song by a mahraganat singer whose name I forget: "We got no choice: it's steal or deal." But not even those two choices could earn you fifty thousand pounds a month. And I knew this was just the beginning. As soon as the real work began, sales would increase and the money would start flowing, and then I'd start getting a cut of the profit, not just a monthly salary.

I hardly knew what to do with fifty thousand pounds. I flagged down a taxi, told the driver to take me to the Four Seasons, and decided to treat myself to a massage, Moroccan bath, scrub, rub-down, and pedicure.

16.

Our sales plan depended on several tracks. I knew we had nightlife, weddings, and bachelor parties in our pocket, so all that remained was to reach the middle class. We had to make them feel part of it, feel that mahraganat music wasn't just for those from a lower social class. We also had to find a way for political players and the national discourse to make use of this energy, this "explosive" power in the mahraganat beat.

So I looked to the stories of American rappers for inspiration. Clearly the way forward was to take Daddy's death and construct some enigmatic rumors. Create an icon. The security forces hadn't yet managed to pin his murder on anyone. But in microbus stations, and in front of elementary and secondary schools, posters showing Bob Marley, Tupac, and Daddy were everywhere. Then came lots of posters, just of Daddy.

Of course, before all this I'd convinced Daddy's grieving mother, and the uncle who descended on the family to provide a male role model, to sign with us in exchange for a big advance. With that, we obtained rights to use all of Daddy's work as we wished. Doctor

Fayza and Mr. Barakat created ways to legitimize mahraganat music and related merchandise, and then they established intellectual property laws. They sued Mahmoud Mataba more than once, and their rights agents hounded DJs who played mahraganat music without obtaining the proper permissions.

There wasn't room anymore for small-time producers like Mataba or Studio Kanka. In this new world, songs weren't the only product of mahraganat music; we also had plans to manufacture clothing and chain necklaces, as well as posters and accessories for cars and tuk-tuks. Next we started producing popular perfumes named after famous songs and mahraganat stars. And before we knew it, the internet was flooded with Daddy's photographs and songs.

Kids loved him. Because he'd died so young, and because his songs were filled with violence and fighting, he came to represent a self-confident soul who had "music from my head to my feet. / Listen to rap or shaabi beat. / I meet the world and bring the heat." People started wearing T-shirts with photos of Daddy opening a flip knife, or with a joint in the corner of his mouth. He became an icon. Everyone wanted to wear clothing with his image printed on it, and there was a resurgence of his older music, too—though this time it wasn't available for free on the internet. You could download it, but it would cost you half a pound.

We started working the back catalog, reissuing and updating the classics. With Fifty, for instance, we produced a new album for Daddy with several star Arab singers. Doctor Haha took care of distribution, and turned these songs into the holy of holies at weddings and dance clubs. The album included songs that married mahraganat music with tunes that Gulf Arabs love, proving that mahraganat music was accepted by stars like Abdallah Belkhair, Hussain Al Jassmi, Waed, and other Gulf singers. We dropped songs that shook the world and lit the roof on fire, including some that blended Bedouin music from the Levant with mahraganat music. Cash was flowing and our power was growing. We also quietly sponsored a group of people who opposed mahraganat songs to speak out against it, ensuring it would stay a subject of debate on talk shows.

I was bidding farewell to my old life, distancing myself from journalism and writing. Now my days were lost to sitting in meetings, arranging ad campaigns, and watching time seep away; to cigarettes; to back pain from not walking or moving around enough; and to Mr. Barakat's advice to walk at least half an hour every day. Doctor Fayza told me to stay in shape and get rid of my paunch, so I went to the gym, downed protein shakes and dietary supplements, and watched my body change. At the same time, my whiskey and cognac consumption increased considerably. And whenever my head began to spin I'd pray for Daddy, for mercy and light a thousand times over, and I thought of Daddy as spears drank my innards, and Indian blades dripped red with my blood.

But even with how far we'd come, I knew that my job here wasn't yet done. Just as with any type of art or music, in order to establish a place in history, mahraganat music needed to gain the acceptance of the authorities. It needed to weave itself into the national fabric, and the threads of that fabric are national discourse on military victories. This, I knew, would be the hardest step yet.

17.

But like the dog who lunges at the river for the reflection of his bone, only to drop the real one into the water, I was soon to learn that you can't have it all. My relationship was falling apart; I was under pressure from work, passion was in its death throes. The girlfriend and I sat down together to find a way forward, searching for any life still beating in our love as it faded. But my phone rang in the middle of our conversation; Mr. Barakat's number appeared, and since I'd been waiting for his call I answered it and told her to hold on a minute.

I turned my back to her as I took the call. Barakat told me that they'd managed to sign a contract with an agency to organize the annual victory celebrations of the Yom Kippur War and the Glorious Revolution. I asked him for details, my pulse quickening as the news I'd been waiting for poured out, and when I finally hung up the phone and turned back around, I couldn't find her anywhere.

18.

Celebrations for the Great Victory and October Revolution involved troops from every branch of the armed forces, in dazzling parades through Grandstand Square. Doctor Haha had written all the music for the celebration; oriental melodies accompanied the troops' choreography as lights from the laser show intersected across the square.

The troops acted out the history of the Egyptian nation: the triumphant struggle of its people and military from the dawn of time until the tree of nationalism, watered by the martyrs' blood, finally bore fruit. The backdrop of the stage was a huge screen, and as the last martyr fell in the troops' choreography, a photograph of Daddy appeared on-screen, standing straight and tall, with his chest thrust forward, giving a military salute, as the Egyptian flag fluttered behind him and musicians played the national anthem. Then suddenly the anthem dropped into a mahraganat track with thumping bass and electronic tabla drum samples, and Fifty appeared onstage, shouting in his harsh, raspy voice: "I dish it out and you lap it up. / I sing the words, now you listen up. / Egypt, my country, will shake you up" to the latest nationalistic mahraganat song: "My Country, My Hero, You Outshine Our Rivals." I'd made sure that during the concert he looked and gestured toward the president every time he said the words "my hero." And sure enough, halfway through the song, the camera zoomed in on the president's face as a simple smile traced its way across his lips. Then there was a wide shot of the front row, filled with senior state officials sitting alongside him. And with my own eyes, I saw the president's left foot tapping to the beat. That, for me, was even more significant than the handshake we'd shared earlier that day.

19.

After months of exhausting work organizing concerts, I decided to spend two days at home. I woke up from a deep sleep, went to the bathroom, washed my hands and face, brushed my teeth, and decided to shave my beard, as I'd noticed a few white hairs.

But first I decided to cook a piece of steak with pasta in bechamel sauce. I walked out of the bathroom and into the kitchen, and headed to the refrigerator to take the meat out and let it thaw while I shaved and showered. I opened the freezer and found a tightly sealed bag containing a piece of paper with the message "You're with Daddy now." I opened the bag and found a cut of meat inside, about half the size of my palm. I prodded it with the tip of my finger. It was deep red, almost black in some places. I raised my finger to my nose. There was a spot of red where I'd touched the meat. It wasn't until I tasted it, my finger deep inside my mouth, that I realized it was a piece of Daddy's liver.

PLACES THAT
HAVE NEVER BEEN

by JOANNA RUOCCO

GEORGE TSAFARAS REACHED THE town of S. in late morning. He saw the sign up ahead and pulled the car off to the side of the road. The side of the road was grassy, shaded by tall trees. He turned the key and the engine stopped. At once, a hush established itself.

George Tsafaras considered himself, among other things, a student of preludes. He took the most care in the moments before the moments that mattered. The windows were down and the morning was right there, all around the car. Nothing moved.

He sat very still and then he got out of the car. There was the sign. It said S. George Tsafaras walked past it, walked into S. In this way, he arrived. Even walking slowly, another man would not have perceived the exact moment he stepped from A., the town through which he'd just lately been driving, into S., the town into which he'd newly arrived. George Tsafaras perceived it.

His greatest talent was for thresholds. This was his trick. He noticed which two distinct objects of the many scattered before him existed in tension, one with the other. Then he stepped between them and through and found he was elsewhere.

From where he stood, in S., there was little to see. The trees closed in upon the road. Above, the sky was bright but mild. In a place like S., which lay in a thin, crooked valley, the wooded hills rising in a jumble of slopes and sudden steep pitches, the sun seems aslant at its zenith and its light is many-angled and does not burn.

The road continued only a dozen yards before it bent sharply and was lost to view.

In the gravel by his shoe, he noticed a scrap of color, a tiny blue cup, the emptied half of a robin's egg. He picked it up.

George Tsafaras had heard explained in many ways the blueness of the robin's egg. The following is the explanation that stuck with him:

> Long ago, the songbirds conspired beneath a screen of
> leaves to overthrow the sky. The robin only pretended
> to go along with the conspirators. As soon as she
> could, she flew up through the trees to give warning.
> The plot was foiled. Ever after, the robin has laid blue
> eggs as a reminder that the sky has also eyes on earth.

George Tsafaras wondered what the songbirds would have done if they'd succeeded, if the sky had fallen, come down like a wave. Would they have found a way to replace all that light with song?

He got back into the car. He drove, and soon a house appeared on his left, yellow, set back from the road. This house, the first house past the town line, was not the first house on George Tsafaras's list. This house was not on his list at all. It was on someone else's then. George Tsafaras drove by the house slowly. A company car was already in the driveway.

*   *   *

Soon, within hours of George Tsafaras's arrival, the town of S., such as it was, would not exist.

All things stop existing at some near or distant point. At some point, all things stop existing, or rather, all things are reconfigured, so drastically they can no longer be recognized. All things that exist at some point exist otherwise, shift kingdoms. Man, clay, heat, light. Darkness. What I will tell you—about the town of S., about George Tsafaras and the company that employed him—is more particular. It involves a protocol for *dislocation*. *Dislocation* is the word favored by the company. The company offers dislocation services to clients—private citizens, foreign nationals, corporations, governments—who wish to take over a town for whatever purpose. The residents of the town—and their livestock, if specified by the client; their pets, if specified by the client; their houses, if specified by the client; their outbuildings and other commercial or public structures, if specified by the client—are removed.

Who contracted with the company for the town of S.? Why was the town of S. desired? Perhaps, if the surface of S. were scraped away, something beneath could be extracted. Or perhaps it was the opposite. There was nothing anywhere—at any depth—in S. that justified its presence. A straight line could be mapped between terminals, if not for S., which represented, in the calculations, interrupted flow, lost profit, the usual atavisms. Or there was another reason, highly personal, or there was no reason.

George Tsafaras did not know what happened when he finished an assignment, when he exited a town through the threshold he'd defined. By the time the residents were collected by the second team, he was gone. If there were sudden tears, scuffles, shots, he did not witness them. Where were they put, these dislocated people? Maybe nowhere. Maybe they entered into the state of dislocation, a space that is not a site, that is between departure and arrival.

Does the world itself change when a person vanishes? When a whole community vanishes? Or is the world afterward the same world it was before, altered only, in one mind or another, from a version held in memory, or dream?

I will follow George Tsafaras through the town of S., although by doing so I will be charting what can't have happened, what his very presence erased.

Around the bend with George Tsafaras. Down the long hill, the river alongside the road then running under it, the road rising to bridge the water, the woods pressing close, and then retreating behind high green fields.

The house he stopped at was very small and shedlike. Beyond the small dooryard, goats were kept in unkind conditions.

—Bud Kelly? he asked when the man came to the door.

—Yes? said the man.

—You drive the town school bus? asked George Tsafaras. This was not in his notes but there in the dooryard were two green bench seats that had come from a school bus.

—I did, said the man, Bud Kelly. Now I repair the seats.

George Tsafaras looked more closely and saw the supplies of this trade scattered around the seats: a heat gun, vinyl patches, vials of vinyl in liquid form, scissors, needle-nose pliers, paint.

—You wouldn't believe what children do to the seats of a school bus, said Bud Kelly. It's not just that they stab into the backs with their pencils. They drop things into the holes, things they want later and try to rip out.

—Like what? asked George Tsafaras, and Bud Kelly looked at him a moment. He was built on a large scale, which made his house appear even more shedlike. Long ago it was perhaps a goat pen and Bud Kelly had displaced the goats. The goats, so far as George Tsafaras could see, did not have a structure of their own. If this was so, where did Bud Kelly live before? With a friend, perhaps. A member of the road crew, a younger man, seemingly without prospects, who, out of nowhere, married and asked Bud Kelly to leave him in private with his wife, although Bud Kelly had been the one to sign the lease, had in a sense taken the younger man in.

For a man like Bud Kelly, thought George Tsafaras, a marriage must be deferred to. He was of that breed of bachelors who backed away from others, who labored—proudly—under the premise that a bachelor was a solvent dangerous to human bonds.

—I'll show you, said Bud Kelly and disappeared into the house.

—Here, he said, and handed George Tsafaras a plastic model of a creature long extinct. The limbs articulated.

—It's nice, said George Tsafaras.

—Keep it, said Bud Kelly. I have dozens. Do you know what I have the most of? What children drop most often into the holes in school bus seats?

George Tsafaras shook his head.

—White crayons, said Bud Kelly. Every white crayon from every pack of crayons ends up in there. Well, why not? Can you think of a use for a white crayon?

Again George Tsafaras shook his head.

—You can't, said Bud Kelly. White crayons are useless. I don't blame the children for getting rid of them. Children are by and large useless, and so they should try to reduce uselessness when they see it. That way things will balance out.

—But the children haven't gotten rid of anything, said George Tsafaras. You have the white crayons. You take them out of the seats. You just said so.

—I've found a use for white crayons, said Bud Kelly, and he narrowed his eyes.

—You won't get it out of me, he said. Who are you? What are you doing here?

The moment had come.

—I'm from the federal police, said George Tsafaras. There's been a crime. A terrible crime. A group of children who boarded their school bus just like on any other morning never arrived at school.

—So? said Bud Kelly.

—We suspect the bus driver, said George Tsafaras. But we don't know where he would have taken them, a whole busload of children. Can you imagine such a thing?

—Come inside, said Bud Kelly, and George Tsafaras went after him into a dim room with a woodstove, a two-burner range, a miniature refrigerator, and a table with one chair. The walls were unfinished and objects were wedged between the studs or balanced on sills. George Tsafaras counted many combs, keys, gloves, rubber balls, wadded papers, tiny necklaces hung from nails. Not a single crayon. But there was another room, the entrance curtained with a sheet. That was perhaps the crayon room.

—Sit, said Bud Kelly.

—Once, said Bud Kelly when George Tsafaras had pulled out the chair and positioned himself, I was driving the school bus through the Notch. Do you know the Notch? It's further up the road, two hairpin turns through the mountain. They blasted the rock to make the road wider but you have to understand the road isn't wide. There's a ravine on one side. A deep one. The drop killed Mark Pike. He was plowing. It was still snowing, still dark, but there was no school delay, the bus had to go out, so he started. We're the ones who found the truck down there, the children and I. We got to the Notch, the snow was suddenly thick on the road, we were sliding, and over the side, far below, we saw the lights of the plow still flashing. The wheels of the bus went right to the edge but I steered us through it.

—You must have been a good driver, said George Tsafaras.

—I went through the Notch twice a day, said Bud Kelly. Even if the weather's good, it takes concentration to drive through with a school bus. The bus is almost too long to make the turns.

—But you did it, said George Tsafaras.

—Twice a day, said Bud Kelly. Not just anyone could. I know other bus drivers who wouldn't want to try it. The drop killed Karl Lieber. That was a little car, in summer. But with Karl Lieber, if it wasn't that, it would have been something else. A tree or a telephone pole.

—I see, said George Tsafaras.

—The time I want to tell you about, said Bud Kelly, it was a winter morning, icy, and I was driving through the Notch, concentrating hard. It took everything I had to keep us on the road. I didn't notice that the bus had gone quiet until it was too late. One boy got his arms around my neck, and another put his thumbs into my eyes. I could feel more of them swarming me, clinging to my arms and legs. It wasn't quiet anymore. Girls were laughing. They were all laughing, boys, girls, screaming to each other. The empty space above the ravine was right there beside us. I hugged the turn. It was instinct. The side of the bus hit the rock wall and that dislodged a few of the boys. I could see again, the metal was sparking on the rock, and then we were out of the Notch and I went right over the shoulder of the road into Ed Gust's field. Ed Gust's dog was coming at us, howling. I opened the bus doors and Ed Gust's dog got onto the bus. The children were all screaming but not laughing anymore, running to the back of the bus, knocking each other down, and Ed Gust's dog was knocking them down too. I let him stay on awhile. When I thought they'd had enough, I dragged him off. That took a while too.

—What happened next? asked George Tsafaras.

—I drove the children to school, said Bud Kelly. And I never let my guard down again. I bought an extra mirror that I mounted on the dashboard. It's important to consider always what's behind you. For instance, you're sitting with your back to the door. What if someone came in silently, someone who meant you harm?

—You'd tell me, ventured George Tsafaras. You'd see and you'd signal to me. We'd work as a team.

Bud Kelly shrugged.

—I always back away from the goats, he said. I don't turn around. They're tied to those tires out there but I've known a goat to eat through rope. They'll eat tires, too, if they can taste the road salt.

George Tsafaras heard a sound behind him. He looked over his shoulder. The door stood open to the morning. There was nothing there. He looked back at Bud Kelly. Bud Kelly was smiling. George Tsafaras smiled too.

—The question you want to ask yourself, said Bud Kelly, is: Where would the children have taken the bus driver?

—That's good, said George Tsafaras, standing. That's very good. We've been working on the case for days and hadn't come to it.

Bud Kelly shrugged again, but in a way that indicated a heightened awareness of his shoulders, which were, in fact, impressive.

—We need your help, said George Tsafaras. Just for the day. My colleagues will come for you. Drive you on the route. You can tell them what you think. You'll be compensated for your time, said George Tsafaras. Of course.

Bud Kelly followed him out into the yard.

—Sure, he said. Send your friends. It won't end well, I don't think. If you want my hunch.

George Tsafaras nodded.

—If the bus is recovered, said Bud Kelly, I get the repairs. The seats won't come through intact. I guarantee it.

—Noted, said George Tsafaras. An hour then. Give or take.

George Tsafaras shifted the plastic figure to his left hand. They shook.

—I'll be here, said Bud Kelly.

In the car, George Tsafaras put the plastic figure on the dashboard. He waved at Bud Kelly as he backed out of the driveway.

Here is something George Tsafaras knew:

If you melt white crayons down in a pot, you can dip each of your fingertips in smooth, transparent wax. Just one layer. The color of your skin comes through. The warmth of your body keeps the wax flexible. No one will notice the difference, not in shade or texture. Yet you won't leave fingerprints no matter what you touch.

Some people, though, like George Tsafaras, don't leave finger-prints anyway. He had no proof of this, but for years, before he worked for the company, he'd worked to remove from houses, not people but their most precious belongings, which he then described in let-ters sent by post the next day or the next year, whenever the mood struck him. At this job, he was self-employed and earned nothing. You could say, then, that it was a hobby.

He let himself into houses like so:

By trying the doors so casually they opened. He did not whistle a tune, but it was as though a tune were being whistled around him. Not an audible tune. More the silent but concordant disposition of materials. He did not wear gloves. He was never caught.

To determine which of a person's belongings is most precious, you can't rely on placement or wear. Some people keep their most precious belongings close to them, either in the open or hidden away, and some keep them at a distance, not in the rooms where they sleep, although that is the most common, but in a hall closet or attic. Some people like to handle their most precious belongings, as they were handled by their previous owners who were also to the people precious, and some people scarcely rest their eyes on them when they go to check that all is well, that their most precious belongings are in their proper spots, in mint condition, safe and unprofaned.

George Tsafaras thought it likely that Bud Kelly, having found a use for white crayons, meant something else altogether. But two uses for white crayons? This was difficult to credit.

What would happen to Bud Kelly when he was driven off by the members of the second team? What would happen to the goats, to the shedlike house, to the lost objects conjured out of school bus seats, to the seats themselves?

Bud Kelly was still in the dooryard. He could see him in the rearview mirror until he took the next curve.

The company that employed George Tsafaras is acephalous. This means it has no headquarters but rather quarters everywhere. Or, you might say, the company is composed of branches without a central trunk.

The first time George Tsafaras went to a company building things did not go as he had hoped.

He had found the building quite by instinct. It was a complex, really, with multiple wings and indifferent landscaping. He let himself in through the garage door where the company cars were serviced. In very little time, he was entering a man's office, making a case for himself.

—Your face is all wrong, said the man when he'd finished. I don't trust it, and I'm a trusting sort. Benefit of the doubt and all that. In fact, it goes beyond that. I used to work in show business. Performers would hire to me to sit in their audiences. Such was the force of my credulity and enthusiasm! It became general. General credulity and enthusiasm. I infected the whole house. Magicians loved me. You've heard of Joe the Magnificent?

—Joe the Magnificent, said George Tsafaras. Yes.

—I got him his start, said the man. It wasn't my fault he turned cocky. I always warned the performers against it, but sometimes they couldn't help it. My power was so strong, you see, they started to trust *themselves*. That's dangerous even with a first-rate talent. How would you rate Joe?

—I can't say, said George Tsafaras. I lack the criteria.

—You don't follow magicians? asked the man.

—No, said George Tsafaras.

—But you've heard of Joe? You'd swear to it?

—I would, said George Tsafaras.

—Do it, said the man.

—I swear, said George Tsafaras.

—There it is, said the man. I don't believe you.

He sighed and leaned across his desk.

—Sometimes the eyebrows can be plucked into a new angle, he said, holding two fingers up to George Tsafaras's forehead and squinting.

—That can do wonders for some faces, he said, but not yours. No, I'm sorry. I won't take an employee on when I can tell at once he's bound to fail. It's not good for the employee, it's not good for me, it's not good for the company. We work in stages, and a problem at the first stage gets compounded.

The man wore a full beard. Some men with this type of beard seem as though they have something to hide while others seem amiable and open-hearted. The man behind the desk fell into the latter category. As no mention of beards had been made, George Tsafaras concluded that in his own case the man did not imagine a beard would be improving.

—I'm willing to solicit a second opinion, said the man. For Joe's sake. Down the hall to your right, third door. Ask for Leonards.

—You want to work for the first team? said Leonards, when George Tsafaras presented himself. This office was smaller than the last, more of a closet. George Tsafaras sat in one chair and Leonards continued in the other.

George Tsafaras nodded, adjusting, as best he could, the angles of his eyebrows. Leonards was clean-shaven and the smallness of his office combined with the books stacked in the corner reinforced an atmosphere of subversion.

—I wouldn't consider you for the second team, or the third, said Leonards, crossing his legs, which necessitated George Tsafaras inching back in his chair. But I like you for the first team. You're unconvincing, but I think that could work to our advantage. Say I hire you. Say I have that power and say I send you out on assignment. You're talking with residents, and they don't fully believe what you're telling them. They *half* believe. They're uncertain. You leave them off-balance. They're unsettled, in need of resolution. The second team arrives with an air of authority and firm decision, and do the residents resist? No, they comply gratefully. They go along with the second team, out of relief more than anything, a sense of restored order. It's unorthodox, granted, but we need to innovate, as a company, or we lose our dynamism. You would be an innovative hire. Of course, I don't have that power, the power to hire. No one does, but I do least of all.

He sighed and laced his fingers together, holding out his elbows as though they were propped on the surface of a desk. Perhaps he had had a desk, and a proper office, until quite recently and was acting out of habit, or perhaps, from the beginning, from his boyhood, he had possessed the skill of a mime. He was able to interact with an imagined desk and so had never needed a real one. Two chairs in a closet sufficed.

—You see, he said. There's some agitation in the company to get rid of the first team altogether. Why ease into the thing at all? Why not send the second team straightaway, no preparation, drag people out kicking and screaming? There might be property damage, that's true, but repairs can be budgeted. And that's assuming the client doesn't want a place leveled, which isn't a reliable assumption by any means. For me, though, the first team is everything. The first team is what makes us different. It's what makes our company uniquely dedicated to humanity, but it goes beyond humanity. There's a fundamental harmony of place, I believe this. Violence creates rupture, and resistance creates blockage. The place itself is damaged. Do you see? When the residents flow from a place, gently, the energy can equilibrate. The client gets a better product. Whatever he decides to do from there is up to him. At that point, it's out of our hands, but that doesn't mean we should abandon our own principles. Do you feel the same? About harmony?

George Tsafaras nodded again and Leonards sighed.

—I like you, he said. If I can ever help you, I will, but I've got my own problems.

Back in the basement, George Tsafaras took a wrong turn and came to a square door at the end of the hall. He let himself through with little difficulty, but when the square door shut behind him, he realized the door had only one side. There was no getting out.

It was true that George Tsafaras did not follow magicians. There was a spell passed down in his family that kept lemon egg soup from curdling. He saw, as a very young child, his mother whisper it over a pot. His mother's soup came out always thick as cream, so smooth and so sour. He found it faintly nauseating and its association with magic turned him off magicians altogether.

It was also true that George Tsafaras had heard of Joe the Magnificent. Joe the Magnificent was from the city, the same city as George Tsafaras. Once, he asked to be locked in the vault of a bank. A crowd gathered to see if he could escape. When the bank officials opened the vault, he was still inside and the crowd abused him roundly. The next day, city papers reported that four blocks of gold had disappeared from the bank, from the very vault in which Joe the Magnificent was locked alone for the better part of an hour. Joe the Magnificent, by then, was nowhere to be found, and, if he hadn't visited the man in the company office, George Tsafaras wouldn't have remembered his name, or that he was briefly a hero in the city. For weeks after the failed escape, people were finding gold coins, stamped with the magician's sigil, in their pockets.

George Tsafaras drove slower and slower. He reached the white church where Sunday service was still in session. Above, on a small hill, the cemetery. A movement caught George Tsafaras's eye.

It was a man, a man moving among the graves. The man wore dark clothing. He held a rifle at the ready, the butt pressed against his shoulder. George Tsafaras pulled his car into the church lot. He was up the hill in an instant.

The man was young, perhaps less than twenty, but aged prematurely by some long harassment. There are individuals who live their whole lives without a moment's peace, and many of these, if they could, would spend their days roving with a rifle, on hilltops or other lonely places, under an overpass, should there be an overpass, along the railroad tracks, behind an industrial park.

Approaching such individuals cannot be advised, and was not by the company. Such individuals should be reported. They should be dealt with decisively, and from a distance, by team members trained in maneuver, strategic and tactical.

If the cemetery had not been encircled by an iron fence in which an iron gate stood open, George Tsafaras would never have run up the hill. As it was, the movement of the young man caught his eye. He saw the gate. He had to go through.it and did.

George Tsafaras was in S. and then he was in a ring within S., in the cemetery, which was different, slightly, from S. generally. In the cemetery, there was more moss, and chamomile, and time passed, as it did in S., but discontinuously. It seemed to George Tsafaras like this: time could not be told in the cemetery on a single clock, but rather, each moment required its own clock.

This was it, he thought. Yes. Time in the cemetery could best be told on an infinite series of stopped clocks. He imagined a hallway lined with such clocks, clocks on both sides, the facing clocks stopped at the same moment, which could be either night or day, and himself going down the hallway, going forward in time but with night and day reversing themselves constantly, from side to side, so that time also shuddered and the intermittent light made it seem that his body, too, existed discontinuously. He wasn't going down the hallway after all. His body was at one point, then another, but no movement between points was possible.

Once in the cemetery, George Tsafaras slowed from a run to a walk, and then he stopped. S. lay outside the cemetery fence and he was inside the fence and so was the young man with the rifle.

A confrontation was inevitable.

* * *

George Tsafaras stood waiting beside a large tree. The young man was slightly higher on the hill, not walking down toward George Tsafaras, but across the hill. George Tsafaras waited quietly but all the same the young man turned. The young man stopped and turned toward him. In that moment, the rifle that he held looked more real than he did, more real than the trees and headstones.

The young man aimed the rifle in his direction. He fired. The shot was loud and echoed between the hills. If you hear a shot, you are most likely alive. The bullet has not passed through your brain, muting the world, reducing the world to a mute red point. Around George Tsafaras the air was warm and agitated. The world was everywhere. No, he was not in the least bit shot. A crow came down hard from a branch overhead and several others flapped into the air.

The young man called to him.

—What are you? he called. An undertaker?

George Tsafaras waited, very still.

—That suit, said the young man. He gestured with the rifle as he spoke. A less discerning interlocutor might have misinterpreted such reflexive movements as preparatory, building to an act of willful murder. Even understood as a kind of tic, the gesturing did not conduce to the easy back-and-forth of normal conversation.

George Tsafaras tried to see himself as the young man would see him, a man in a black suit, his contours stark and rectilinear, as though he'd been cut out from a different background. He did not belong in S., that much was obvious. But where did he belong? What was the background, the scene from which he'd been snipped? The young man's own black clothing was made of canvas, canvas coat, canvas pants, heavily paneled and grommeted.

George Tsafaras said: I'm not an undertaker.

The young man approached. He nudged the dead crow with the side of his boot.

—It was a good shot, he said. There was never a chance I'd hit you.

—I didn't think so, said George Tsafaras.

The young man turned his eyes on the other crows, watching them settle back down on the hill below.

—They don't forget faces, he said. If you kill one, the others remember you. Let me show you something.

The young man had an erratic but deliberate way of walking and George Tsafaras matched it. They moved along a series of short diagonals between headstones. The headstones on this part of the hill were white, thin, old, streaked with gray lichen. Their surfaces were granular and wordless. The headstones affected George Tsafaras, who had always had a sensitivity to marble, which even newly quarried expressed somehow the poignancy of ruins. Marble appeals to some, often the tone-deaf, who lack access to music, that most ephemeral architecture. George Tsafaras was among these. When he sang in the choir as a tiny boy, the nuns had flushed him out, hunted among the rows of children until they found him, at the end of the second riser. They rapped his knuckles and poked him with the heads of pins until he learned to move his lips to the psalm without sound.

The young man came to a patch of dirt and squatted beside it. George Tsafaras squatted also.

—Those scratches there, said the young man. What are they? Can you tell?

The scratches were frenzied and senseless. George Tsafaras studied them.

—A drawing, said the young man. What does it look like to you?

He moved his finger above the scratches, tracing a shape in the air.

—It's a crow, said George Tsafaras.

—It's me, said the young man. It's how they draw me. It's all over, this exact drawing. They recognize me from it, ones I've never seen before. That's the gun.

He indicated the longest, straightest scratch. His rifle was across his knees.

George Tsafaras thought:

(1) Scuffle with young man. Young man disarmed. No need to radio. Regular removal.

(2) Scuffle with young man. Failure to disarm. Beaten with rifle butt (self). Regain consciousness. Radio. Forced removal/death of young man.

(3) No scuffle. Radio. Forced removal/death of young man.

(4) No scuffle. No radio. Escape of young man.

The best outcome seemed to him the least likely, the second-best outcome the second least likely, and so on. Meanwhile the young man was speaking.

—When I drew animals in school, said the young man, as a kid, kindergarten, first grade, the animals looked more like people. Bears standing on two legs in front of houses, smiling. You can picture what I mean?

—Of course, said George Tsafaras, and the young man stared at him. He had been humored in the past, George Tsafaras could see, and the humoring party had not come out of it unscathed.

He added: I drew mice in striped shirts. Also upright.

—Smiling? asked the young man.

—I think so, said George Tsafaras. Yes.

—But you've never seen such a thing in real life? Animals smiling?

—Not mice, certainly, said George Tsafaras. They're more inquisitive.

—The noses make you think that, said the young man. Mice have those noses they hold up.

They did. George Tsafaras nodded.

—You don't know what mice are thinking, continued the young man. Even if a mouse smiled, you couldn't say it was happy. Like trout. Trout look like they're suffering, even in the water. Have you seen the faces of trout?

—In fish markets, mostly, said George Tsafaras. Where the grimaces correspond to circumstance.

—Their faces are always that way, said the young man. That's what I'm saying. There's no correspondence. With animals, expressions don't mean anything. But I drew smiling bears, and you drew smiling mice.

—In striped shirts, said George Tsafaras. Yes.

—That's how people are, continued the young man. He spit something gray.

—To people, everything is people.

There was a pause and George Tsafaras made a nonverbal noise of encouragement.

—Well, said the young man. That's how crows are too. To crows, everything is crows. A person isn't a person. A person is a kind of crow. You have to put yourself in a crow's mind to understand. Not the human idea of a crow's mind but a crow's idea of a crow's mind. Look at that drawing again. Try to see it like they do.

George Tsafaras looked again.

—You can't tell it's me? A crow's version?

—No, he said.

The young man stood abruptly. He scuffed and stamped the dirt.

—That's the worst part, he said. No one can tell. I went years without noticing. I saw that drawing all over, in mud, in ice, in bark, in barn boards, everywhere, but I saw it like a person sees it. Then one day I saw it differently. I recognized myself.

George Tsafaras stood too. He thought: (1), (2), (3), (4), and again, but in a different order, and then he reviewed each item, appending additional outcomes.

The sliver of valley stretched below, the road, the church, the curved, bright field. Straight across that narrow open space, green mountains rose to close the vista. From even a small distance, deciduous trees en masse take on the smeared or pointillistic look of oils, while pines are calligraphic, inked, conveying to the eye a certain rectitude. If the choice were presented to him, George Tsafaras would live among pines, but this choice hadn't been and wouldn't be, he was almost certain.

The young man's perturbation was increasing. He lifted the rifle.

—They got to me, he said. They're inside my head now. I see how I see, but I also see how they see. I can't stop it.

George Tsafaras followed the rifle back and forth with his eyes.

—My only hope, said the young man, is that one of them in particular is behind it. A leader. I kill the leader and the rest of them scatter. Get confused. Lose their nerve. It could happen like that. They make it hard though. Bait you with a big one, or one with a scissor beak or a blind eye. A white tail feather. Something obvious. That's never it. I go for the ordinary ones now. That one, for example. That one farthest on the right.

The young man pointed with the rifle.

—Or it's not a crow at all, said the young man, turning face, body, gun toward George Tsafaras.

—The leader, he said. They could be that devious. The leader isn't what we would call a crow.

Of all the things the young man had said, George Tsafaras liked this least. It caused him to increase the speed of his thinking, or try to. If he grabbed the barrel of the rifle and forced it down, the bullet would lodge harmlessly in earth. The rifle would become, not harmless exactly, but less dynamic in its modes of attack. But only if the young man fired at that first contact, squeezed his fingers convulsively on the trigger. The young man might not react that way at all. He might fight back without firing, the rifle still loaded, a live thing, complex and lethal. Then would come the moment when one man or the other broke free.

—It's too soon for that, said George Tsafaras. You're playing right into their hands with those speculations. They want you off balance. They want you to see any creature as a threat.

—You think the leader is a crow?

—I do, said George Tsafaras. Definitely. Maybe not that one there, on the right. But one of them.

The young man turned again, rifle swinging with him.

—You're right, he said. Besides, I have to start somewhere.

—Can you wait, then, until I'm down the hill? asked George Tsafaras. Before you shoot?

The young man did not answer for a long moment. He was considering, or taking aim.

—Maybe, he said. If you don't startle them.

Luckily, for George Tsafaras quickness and lightness of step went together. He passed the crows at a run and they only hopped, wings folded. There were dozens of them ranged between the headstones, black with black shadows on the sunlit grass.

George Tsafaras went out through the gate in the fence but felt no shift in anything at all. The gate, as is sometimes the case with cemetery fences, was a threshold in one direction only. There had to be a second gate, another gate set somewhere in the fence, a gate for exiting, but looking back at the cemetery he didn't see this second gate.

By exiting through the first gate, the gate through which he entered the cemetery, he had only, he realized, reentered the cemetery. He had brought the cemetery with him, brought the cemetery through the gate, like inverting a sock. As he traveled farther from the cemetery on the hill, S. would be turning inside out, pulled through the ring that was within it.

This realization mattered only to George Tsafaras, who had invented it. Company employees at that very moment were ranging themselves along the perimeter of S., making a physical cordon of electrified wire. They were erecting blinds, deflecting public roads, cutting the lines of communication. These employees had been given instructions and coordinates to work from. They did not care if S. was, in a sense, a ghost town, a place that, without the blinds, without the roads, was nonetheless already unreachable, always at the corner of the eye.

An excerpt from

YOUR
NAME HERE

by HELEN DEWITT *and* ILYA GRIDNEFF

IT STARTED SO WELL before it all went so horribly wrong. P2C2E,
says Rushdie, anticipating text-messaging by a decade. Process Too
Complicated To Explain. A 2C2E life is not really minimalist or
Beckettian, it's just too fucking complicated for a soundbite. Rushdie
was writing a children's book (*Haroun and the Sea of Stories*, o ignorant
reader, o kafir). 2FC2E was too X-rated for the target audience. So he
relied on the intelligence of those readers above the age of consent
to fill in the invisible blank.

It is 2FC2E. It is *War and Peace* meets *The Wandering Jew* meets
A Suitable Boy meets *À la recherche du temps perdu* meets *The Forsyte
Saga* meets *The Cairo Trilogy* meets the Jalna saga of Mazo de la Roche
(trust me, you don't want to know). But this is the age of Aladdin
Stuffit Expander. Perhaps a 500,000-word substitute for a sleeping
pill can be compressed. The imaginative reader can turn to Aladdin.
The unimaginative reader can expand his horizons by reading *War*

and Peace, *The Wandering Jew*, *A Suitable Boy*, *À la recherche du temps perdu*, *The Forsyte Saga*, *The Cairo Trilogy* and *La comédie humaine* (the sort of reader whose horizons can be expanded by the Jalna saga of Mazo de la Roche should sell this book now on Amazon Marketplace, go on, do it, permission to leave the class granted).

Imagine a book doing for Arabic, Farsi, Turkish, Kurdish, Azeri, Armenian, Uyghur, Urdu, Pashtu, Mandarin, Russian, Ukrainian, Hebrew and and and what *The Lord of the Rings* did for Quenya, Sindarin, Telerin, Doriathrin, Nandorin, Adûnaic, Khuzdul, the Black Speech, Westron, Orcish, Entish and and and and and. Tolkien referred to inventing languages as his secret vice; he opened a Finnish grammar, fell in love with the language and wanted to appropriate it, he loved Welsh, Latin, Anglo-Saxon, the Norse of the sagas, Hebrew, did not care for French. He believed that languages were marked by history, and invented Middle-earth to give his languages the marks of violence, loss, exile. Quenya and Sindarin (two Elvish languages) are the only two which are useable—that is, it is possible to write in them if you don't want to talk about credit derivatives or leather fetish lesbian triangles. Tolkien did not provide a comprehensive grammar and vocabulary of every language spoken by every bit player. No. What he created was something more startling: desire. The language of the Wood Elves, Nandorin, is represented by only 30 words or so. The reader constructed by Tolkien is consumed with longing for the nonexistent language of these nonexistent wood dwellers.

The final volume of *The Lord of the Rings* was published in 1955, a year before Suez. Tolkien died in 1973, the year of the oil crisis. By 2003, the year of the invasion of Iraq, the books had sold 100 million copies.

So imagine the book of an alter-Tolkien, creating desire for the languages of the Middle East rather than Middle-earth. Readers who were 13 in 1973 would have been 31 at the time of the Gulf War, 41 in 2001. Whatever events of terror might have been committed in that possible world, it's unlikely that interrogators in it would be holding people in Guantánamo Bay four years after the event for want of competent Arabists to interrogate them.

OK, you say, I imagine the book. I imagine 12-year-olds hauled off to Cuba and released after four days rather than four years. But I sort of liked John Lennon better?

OK. Here's a piece of advice. Why not borrow *Jalna*, by Mazo de la Roche, from your local library? I think you'd enjoy it.

2FC2E, I was once young and enthusiastic and naive.

I first read *The Hobbit* when I was nine. The library of castoff paperbacks in a rotting palace in Mardan had nothing else in the series; I moved on to *The Spy Who Came In From the Cold*. My parents (as I then referred to them in my young, naive, unalienated way) were ending a marriage of smashed chandeliers, airborne dinner services, grand pianos hurtling down marble steps to the bottom of swimming pools. I went back to the beginning of *The Hobbit*. I was given *The Lord of the Rings* for my tenth birthday; I opened the first page under the doting eyes of stewardesses en route to Dakar, finished it under further dotage two months later on a plane to Rangoon. I went back to the beginning of *The Hobbit*.

A succession of steps, recruited for disinclination to smash chandeliers, were discarded for disinclination to smash chandeliers.

So it was not Beckettian, no, it was not very Bauhaus.

What did my father do? He was a simple carpet salesman.

My mother had picked up the carpet business from my father.

Here, however, at the threshold of a philosophical analysis of identity, it seems appropriate to insist on the face it wears and turns on daily life— namely repetition as such, the return of sameness over and over again, in all its psychological desolation and tedium: that is to say, neurosis. In that limited appropriation which Adorno makes of Freudian conceptuality... neurosis is simply this boring imprisonment of the self in itself, crippled by its terror of the new and unexpected, carrying its sameness with it wherever it goes, so that it has the protection of feeling, whatever it might stretch out its hand to touch, so that it never meets anything but what it knows already. Fredric Jameson, *Late Marxism*. Father, a reliable source informs me, of seven. Meaning what?

Meaning a business opportunity.

The tedium of *The Two Towers* gets worse each time. Everyone cracks sooner or later. What do they do?

One thing they could do is turn to the real world for the things they love in Tolkien. The real world has its institutions, and they have no place for Elvish sagas; they also have no place for the *Iliad* and *Odyssey*, the *Kalevala*, the *Mabinogion*, *Beowulf*, *Egil's Saga*, the *Nibelungenlied*, the *Chanson de Roland*, the *Morte d'Arthur*, *Gilgamesh*. They have no use for literary languages. The addict could reason as follows: Much as I love Tolkien, I do not think his Elvish poetry beats Homer AND Beowulf AND AND AND AND so I will learn Greek in Boca Raton Anglo-Saxon in Shanghai Finnish in Tegucigalpa Welsh in Alice Springs.

They could. What they normally do is try another fantasy series (it has to be better than reading *The Two Towers* again). It's like trying to get drunk on cough syrup, but the idea of turning to a real thing is too alien. So the fantasy genre accounts for 10 percent of all books sold, an unreliable source claims.

Or a reader might raise his head from the book. He sits on a bed in a tiny bedroom surrounded by paperbacks. He thinks: I sit here reading about adventure; why don't I walk out the door? Sometimes he has spent too long in the Land of the Lotus-Eaters; he takes a step to the door, picks up another book, returns to the bed. Sometimes he walks through the door. He hitchhikes, backpacks. Yes he does.

Another business opportunity.

Or a reader might raise his head from the book. He will run out of money fast if he walks out the door. So he goes online, writes around, lines up a job teaching English in Kyoto or Bangkok or Riyadh or Kiev. He speaks English to people who speak English, and he teaches English to people who can afford to pay to learn English. He acquires two or three girlfriends or boyfriends. Perhaps he sees prostitutes, or perhaps he's a gentleman.

Another business opportunity.

Rather a lot of third person masculine singulars, you may think. Yes.

But let's say a reader is a 12-year-old female smart-ass, the type of heroine popular with Mistah Rushdie and Mistah Pullman. Popular, in other words, with writers who can keep her safely on the page (they don't have to live with her). This reader notices that Mistah Multi-Culti Rushdie is not denting his very own personal sales by cluttering the page with Hindustani (except in transliteration, we spit on transliterations). She notices that Professah Tolkien cluttered his very own personal pages with his very own personal languages and sold in the millions. Which means that millions of people could pick up Elvish in a mass market paperback while real bombs were falling on real people in Afghanistan and Iran and Iraq and other places whose languages cannot be picked up in a mass market paperback.

She would like to leave home, but being a 12-year-old smart-ass she has of course read *Lolita*, *Zazie dans le métro* and *Candide*. White market labour is closed to 12-year-olds, which leaves drug dealing, theft, prostitution with paedophiles and a literary career. She does not feel up to inventing a language (though she does dodge Stockholm syndrome vis-à-vis legal guardians through a diary written in code, a cunning mixture of Chinese characters and Arabic verb forms).

But wait a minute. How did the Taliban get into power in the first place? The Ayatollah Khomeini—how did this gibbering lunatic escape exile in Paris to hand out death warrants on Rushdie from Tehran? Saddam Hussein—wasn't he once the good guy? If Iran had had the decency to switch to Quenya in 1955 the CIA could have drawn on a pool of linguists to spy on it. It didn't. Afghanistan was equally uncooperative. Iraq also failed to see the light. The CIA simply failed to adapt to wily opponents who continued to converse amongst themselves in their native tongues. Hinc illae lacrimae.

So a 12-year-old smart-ass reasons as follows. There are two possibilities:

> 1. Readers are not incurably neurotic. They do not necessarily read to escape the real world. A vast untapped market could be entranced by the glamour of Arabic, Farsi, Chinese (whichever has most recently enchanted the youthful smart-ass) in the way that one once was entranced by JRRT. So there is money to be made by writing a runaway bestseller, yes, and there is ALSO money to be made by persuading the CIA to fund the project, as increasing the pool of potential intelligence-gatherers in languages of importance to national security.

> 2. Readers are, in fact, ostriches. They have problems of their own and they read to forget about them. Lovely glamorous Arabic would not only not make them forget their problems, it would remind them that there are all kinds of problems they can do nothing about. So there might be a small untapped market of mute inglorious McJob-bound Miltons, but

there is no money to be made by writing a runaway
bestseller. No. But there is money to be made by
persuading the CIA to fund the project, as increasing
the pool of potential intelligence-gatherers in
languages of importance to national security.

I took up my pen. I began to write.
Pride goeth before a fall.

In 1992 my father married a new 29-year-old. The carpet business
had taken him to Hong Kong; she had gone with him, putting her
career on hold. She had a degree in political science from the LSE
but it was not possible to work. She had been writing chick lit to
have her own income.

There are servants but she knows no Cantonese.

There's a dinner. It would be gauche to ask for a knife and fork.
Lucy fumbles with chopsticks.

The carpet business will be discussed later, behind closed doors.
Meanwhile Lucy's cousin Simon talks about *Bat-Mitzvah Boy*, a runaway
bestseller which has started a craze for Hebrew, Aramaic and tapdancing.

With the wisdom of hindsight we can, perhaps, agree that, could
we have replaced that generation of tapdancers with Arabists, stupid-
ities and crassnesses might have been avoided. The world was younger.

So. *Bat-Mitzvah Boy*. The toe-curlingly awful *Bat-Mitzvah Boy*.

Simon had come across five chapters of an early draft in 1988.
Its then penniless author, Max Wojczuk, was working the graveyard
shift at Curzon Street Kinko's; Simon had had a last-minute rush job
for Sotheby's, had begun idly reading the repro op's MS, had become
completely *engrossed*, had *begged* to be allowed to take it away. He had
shown the chapters excitedly to his boyfriend, who had shown them

excitedly to his closest friend, an entertainment lawyer. A movie option had been bought for £500! A publisher had picked up the world rights and made $1 million! So these friends were sitting on the movie rights to a runaway bestseller!

My wine glass is being filled along with everyone else's because Lu's Cantonese is not up to the countermand. The entertainment lawyer dips a spring roll in sweet and sour sauce; red lips close on the greasy skin, and all the while the snake charmer weaves his spell:

—Sometimes a film is absolutely *of* its time, yet *ahead* of its time, a film that will be cherished for years to come. We felt at once that *Bat-Mitzvah Boy* would be one of that rare breed, a film that would live in the hearts of generations—a *Wizard of Oz* for the 21st century.

He fixes his Bambi eyes on Peter Chan, a very major player in the carpet trade. $50 mil would be nothing to Peter Chan, and so the silver tongue speaks on:

—I think part of its extraordinary appeal is the way it plugs into a very powerful nostalgia people are only half aware of. We've seen the whole *gamut* of self-aware, *sophisticated* period musicals, from *Cabaret* to *Grease* to *Saturday Night Fever*, from *Oh What a Lovely War* to *A Chorus Line*; we've seen the whole superhero cinematization of the comic book movement, which looks so obvious now it's hard to believe someone had to *think* of it. In a couple of years people will be thinking—*tapdancing*. Why did no one think of tapdancing *before*? Where's *our* Astaire and Rogers? Where's *our* Gene Kelly? There's the whole *glamour* of it, and with it the *knowledge* we have now of the anguish *behind* the glamour, Rogers' shoes filling with blood, a sort of savage reworking of *The Little Mermaid*, in its original, cruel, unDisneyfied version. And then, of course, there's the whole charm of the troupe of seven children, a sort of *reprise* of *The Sound of Music*, only with tapdancing. And at the same time it avoids that *syrupy*, *saccharine* sentimen*tality*, there's this wonderful *black humour*, this sort of glorious Mel Brooks irreverence, that you really do want for kids today, the *last* thing we want is some kind of Shirley Temple dimpling and twinkling *winsomeness*, a little ringleted *monstrosity*, it's a film with a heart, but one that doesn't buy its emotion cheaply.

When I first read *Bat-Mitzvah Boy* the thing it brought to mind was the unbearable poignancy of those old clips of the Jackson 5. Those sharp, tight routines still work; the sheer professionalism is a joy. The 5 are never embarrassing; they're not dated by the Afros and flares the way the Osmonds are by shag haircuts and skinny rib T-shirts. But now we know the price that was paid for that slick perfectionism, its picture of Dorian Gray stares out at us from all the tabloids. *Bat-Mitzvah Boy* captures that brutal dichotomy.

I am profoundly convinced that *Bat-Mitzvah Boy* is a film that can showcase some *truly exceptional talent*. When you've got a whole slew of good parts for dancers you're in a *very* strong position—there are so *few*, and a dancer's career is so *brief*—and there's some *wonderful* talent out there. And of course when you have a role for a child—we were thinking perhaps Lourdes Leon, she'd be perfect in so many ways, and Madonna's been very involved with Judaism recently so the whole tapdancing family in flight from the Holocaust slash boy helps sisters to get religious rite of passage previously denied, the whole wonderful package is very much *centred* on matters that are of immense *importance* to Madonna. Then there's the way the film *shares* the children's engagement with the Hebrew text, which is *simply extraordinary*, something that would have been *unthinkable* 50, even 20 years ago. But what we see these days is that audiences have a desperate *longing* for *authenticity*, something the beancounters simply hadn't the imagination to *recognize*. And of course this opens up a whole *range* of merchandise possibilities for the film that go *well* beyond the normal stuffed toys, dolls, lunchboxes and what have you.

Peter Chan says that's very interesting and do they have any particular actors in mind.

—Well, of course it's early days to lock any actors in place, we
don't want to present the director with a paint-by-number assignment, it's simply not that kind of film, it needs a director who's
passionate about the *project*, it's really not for Sam and me to *dictate*,
but I think any director who really understood what it was all about
would want to *talk* to Madonna—we *very* much want that unerring
instinct for the postmodern postproduced MTV generation.

Peter Chan says that's very interesting and has Madonna shown
any interest in the project.

—Well, *yes*, as a matter of fact. We've had an *inkling*. We're *not*
making any *promises*, and we're *very* much not taking anything for
granted, but we're *very* much not ruling anything out.

I sit in silence. My glass is filled a second time. Peter Chan and
the other carpeteers make polite noises and now Sam is talking about
the contractual side. In *Haroun and the Sea of Stories* there are villains
with shiny bald heads and yellow checked pants, but this is just a
guy in chinos and a blue button-down shirt, no tie.

He is explaining about options, the actor's contract will typically
give the producer an option to use him again for the next movie or
the next two movies at the same flat fee, you could potentially have
that kind of contract on a Julia Roberts pre–*Pretty Woman* and then
make *Pretty Woman*.

—So maybe the guy wants to work on another picture, now he's
got all kinds of offers, you might come to an agreement, you might
let somebody else use the guy in return for compensation. Or let's
say the guy says Fuck you, I won't do it, sue me, you might say Look,
OK, we know the kind of offers you're getting, the contract says
you get $150,000, we'll make it $300,000. But you're still getting
a million-dollar actor at way below market value. Because the thing

of it is, you're giving someone their break. If they don't like it, there are thousands more where they came from, there are thousands out there waiting tables who would jump at the chance to be in a movie that will be seen, instead of maybe some student production at NYU that maybe gets screened at Sundance if it's lucky. Heh heh.

Chopsticks convey a wonton erratically to the waiting mouth. Peter Chan says that's interesting. The mouth continues:

—So the thing you have to understand is, using a big star is not the only way to make money. But you have to get it right. You want name recognition because that really helps with the distribution. But maybe the big thing about that movie will be somebody who's just getting their break, because there is some amazing talent out there. So if you have that combination, if you find the right project, and you find the right director, and hopefully you find some great talent, you can have a movie that can really take off for not a lot of money. And then that puts you in a position to leverage the money you make into more money, because you can use that actor you gave a break to. And we definitely have a great project.

Isn't there an insect, would it be a dung beetle, that rolls up little pellets of dung? The voice rolls dung pellets into the ear.

—Also, when you have a project that has a great part for a kid, that has incredible potential. You saw *Home Alone*, you remember that incredible kid, Macaulay Culkin, or Tatum O'Neal in *Paper Moon*, the movie has the potential to be iconic.

A wonton punctuates.

—Plus, when you have a project that has a great part for a kid, that puts you in a very strong position. Because on the one hand the parents and the representation of a child actor definitely know, or if the parents don't know the representation definitely knows, but usually the parents know, that the kid has a sell-by date. Whatever the kid has going for him may or may not survive the transition into adulthood. But also, if the kid has a genuine talent, if it's not just a cute kid, people with the kid's interests at heart want to see that develop. But the typical kid or teen movie has very limited crossover potential as a basis for an adult career. So if you have a project that has a really great part, an acting part, for a kid, you are offering some kid the chance not to retire at the age of 15. If you think about what *Taxi Driver* did for Jodie Foster, that's what you are offering the kid. So you really just have to make sure the investor understands that, that the potential to leverage that into a profit is phenomenal.

The carpeteers say that's interesting, that's very interesting, and my glass is filled a third time, and I break the silence.

—The thing that beggars comprehension, I say, is why the CIA haven't funded similar projects for Arabic, Farsi, Russian, Mandarin, any language they might want to spy in. I should have thought it was obvious to the meanest intelligence. They subsidised Horizon for years, didn't they? Surely it's the easiest thing in the world to slash an operative or two and buy up a few Tolkiens and also-rans.

The guests perform an out-of-the-mouths-of-babes bonding ritual.

—I don't think it's quite that simple, Rachel, says Lu, not because she thinks it's complicated but because she is unnerved by hearing *beggars comprehension* and *I should have thought* and *obvious to the meanest intelligence* from the mouth of a 16-year-old.

—Or if the Americans won't do it, what about the Brits? With all due respect, the present system is simply asking for a Philby.

—I'd have thought coming up with a suitable vehicle might present problems, even supposing—

—But that's easy. What about something like *The Name of the Rose?* A historico-philosophical thriller set in 10th-century Baghdad about Ibn Muqlah, father of Arabic calligraphy, whose right hand was amputated in punishment for political machinations, the sort of thing that could hardly fail to be an international blockbuster, thereby increasing the pool of potential Arabists by a million or so. Or a PKD-Fuentes-inspired alternative universe sort of book, in which the Moors kept Granada and conquered the New World? Or one could take a leaf out of the books of Kafka, Borges and Zweig, one could have a novella in which a prisoner sees letters appear one at a time in his breath on the mirror

The 16-year-old brain is all-seeing, all-knowing.

—Yes, but it's all very well to throw balls in the air, Christ, as soon as people hear you're a writer they start bombarding you with all the brilliant ideas they've had for a book, there's all the difference in the world between having an idea and the actual hard slog of writing. Let's cut to the chase, says Lu. Have you ever actually written a book?

—Skoodles, I say, dividing the actual number by five, and my glass is on empty and Yu Peng leaps to refill it.

—The one about Ibn Muqlah is probably the one that would be most attractive to the CIA, though. I think if we were to do for Arabic what Indiana Jones did for archaeology we'd see a dramatic improvement in our relations with the Arab world, and I'd like to think there's some money in it for me for making this important contribution to world peace, so if anybody here happens to know somebody in a position to make it worth my while I'd be only too thrilled.

—But that's amazing, says Lu, suddenly not tense, because it's too ridiculous. You must show me one sometime, and now I think we're ready for coffee.

So what a little player. What a wheeler and dealer. Rushdie's little smart-ass is called Miss Blabbermouth, not without reason.

Later people would hear of these books and imagine that any one of them could be an easy second novel. These are friendless orphans, alone in the world.

* * *

Lucy said nicely the next day that she'd love to see a few chapters.

—OK, but don't lose them, this is my only copy because all the Arabic has to be written in by hand.

Lucy smiles, reassures. Reads.

Frowns.

Smiles.

—I love this. I love this. I don't think it's publishable, unfortunately, I think all the Arabic would put people off, but there's a wonderful gift for storytelling. I think there could be a movie in this. I really think so. What I'd like to do is option it so I can develop the project.

This is not the fast track to a defence budget slush fund that I'd been hoping for.

—I was thinking of $500 for five years, it may take a while what with the book being unpublished and me being stuck in Honkers.

If you are 16 people think $500 is a wonderful piece of luck. It is not possible to ask for more money, though $500 is at least $2,500 shy of even an indie lowest-of-the-low-budget minimum.

Lu got a contract off Sam that she said was standard language. It included a clause about novelization rights.

Baby: How is it possible to include novelization rights in a contract that is for the movie rights to a novel?

A 16-year-old smart-ass is no match for a 29-year-old fuckwit. She weeps, she sobs, she breaks down, let's not talk about it.

If she needs a five-year option (because of having put her career on hold in Hong Kong), rather than the normal 18-month option with right to extend, it is not possible to ask for the industry norm. If she looks at three chapters of another book and falls in love with them and thinks this too could make a wonderful film and offers $250 there is nothing to be done.

* * *

Perhaps you can see the sort of precedent this sets.

Now suppose you have a rapidly expanding kinship system. The parents acquire blameless spouses, behave unforgivably, are forgiven, move on. The number of people who have heard of the runaway best-seller *Bat-Mitzvah Boy* and the friends who optioned it early on is very large. The number of people who think they can make a movie if they have the right project is not small. The number of people who have not been treated appallingly is negligible. So there are quite a lot of people magnanimously asking to see anything you have written and falling in love with anything you show and making an offer of a few hundred dollars which cannot be refused.

Perhaps you can understand this. One way people show it is not just a business relationship is by offering friendly sums of money. Another way is by talking about their problems.

Perhaps you can understand this. A young smart-ass who succeeds in flogging a literary property for a businesslike sum of money can swan into a university and close the door on the crisis-ridden kinship system. A smart-ass who is unable to live on friendly sums of money may weasel herself into the Sorbonne (1994), Berkeley (1995), the American University of Beirut (1997), but there are disappearances, breaches of the social fabric, no degree.

This is something you may not understand. Suppose you give someone a friendly deal, a five-year option for $500. Suppose people talk and talk and talk to the point where the mind cracks up, there is a disappearance or some other breach of the social fabric. The fact that you gave someone a very friendly deal does not mean that this person will not be talking about institutions and electro-shock therapy.

So this is something you may not know that's well worth knowing. If you want to avoid institutions and electro-shock therapy, friendly deals are not the way to go.

CONTRIBUTORS

ABRAHAM ADAMS is a poet and artist based in Gainesville, Florida. His work has been exhibited internationally and published as the books *Ambulance Chasers* (MIT Press, 2022), *Nothing in MoMA* (Punctum Books, 2018), and *Before* (Inpatient Press, 2016). A graduate of Hampshire College, Brown University, and the Royal College of Art, he teaches at the University of Florida and was recently a finalist for the Oxford Poetry Prize.

CAROLINE BEIMFORD's stories and essays have appeared in *Zoetrope: All-Story*, the *Oxford American*, *Electric Literature*, and elsewhere. She holds an MFA in fiction from the University of Arkansas and has received support from the Bread Loaf Writers' Conference, the Sewanee Writers' Conference, the New York State Summer Writers Institute, the Arkansas Arts Council, and Millay Arts. She currently teaches writing at MIT.

REBEKAH BERGMAN's debut novel, *The Museum of Human History*, was longlisted for the VCU Cabell First Novelist Award and received a special citation from the Philip K. Dick Award. Her writing appears in *Electric Literature*, *The Rumpus*, *Literary Hub*, *Joyland*, and other publications. She lives in Rhode Island with her family.

T. C. BOYLE is a longtime contributor to *McSweeney's*. He is the author of thirty-two books of fiction, most recently the environmental novel *Blue Skies* (2023), a central proposition of which inspired "Cold Summer." His new novel, *No Way Home*, will be published next year.

HELEN DEWITT was born in a suburb of Washington, DC. Daughter of American diplomats, she grew up mainly in Latin America. She went to Oxford to study classics for a BA and DPhil before leaving academia to write. She is the author of *The Last Samurai* (hailed by *Vulture* as "the Best Book of the Century"), as well as *Lightning Rods*, *The English Understand Wool*, and *Some Trick*. She lives in Berlin.

CAMONGHNE FELIX is the author of the memoir *Dyscalculia: A Love Story of Epic Miscalculation* (One World, 2023) and the poetry book *Build Yourself a Boat* (Haymarket Books, 2019), which was longlisted for the 2019 National Book Award in Poetry, shortlisted for the PEN Open Book Award, and shortlisted for the Lambda Literary Award. Her work has appeared in *The New Yorker*, the *Academy of American Poets*, the *Harvard Review*, *Literary Hub*, *Vanity Fair*, *New York Magazine*, and elsewhere.

ILYA GRIDNEFF was born and raised in Sydney, Australia. He has worked for the London tabloids, lived in Papua New Guinea for the Australian Associated Press, in South Sudan for the Associated Press, and in East Africa for *Bloomberg*. Now based in Toronto, he covers Canada for the *Financial Times*. There are several manuscripts that remain on the back burner.

ELISABETH JAQUETTE is a translator from the Arabic and the executive director of Words Without Borders. Her translation of *Minor Detail* by Adania Shibli was a finalist for the National Book Award for Translated Literature and longlisted for the International Booker Prize. Her other translations have been shortlisted for the Warwick Prize for Women in Translation, the Saif Ghobash Banipal Prize for Arabic Literary Translation, and the TA First Translation Prize. She lives in Tucson, Arizona.

JAC JEMC teaches creative writing at UC San Diego and serves as the faculty director of the Clarion Writers' Workshop. She is the author of five books of fiction, most recently *Empty Theatre* and *False Bingo*. She was a 2023 Guggenheim Fellow and a recent finalist for the California Book Award.

MENG JIN is the author of the novel *Little Gods* and the story collection *Self-Portrait with Ghost*. She is currently writing a fake memoir.

JAMES KAELAN is an innkeeper and the author of two novels: *We're Getting On*, which grew into a spruce tree if you planted it; and *999 Years of Peace* (excerpted here), of which only 132 copies were ever made, and which is currently sneaking from reader to reader like Soviet-era samizdat. His third novel, *Fragment*, likes scary walks through drainage canals and a boozy lunch, and is currently in search of an unconventional publishing relationship. Track him down at jameskaelan.com if you want to know more!

PATRICK KECK is a cartoonist living in Portland, Oregon. His books include *Little Tomb* (2019); *Peepers* (2021); *Dream of the Bat* (2022), in collaboration with Josh Simmons; and, in collaboration with Thomas Stemrich, *Crusher Loves Bleeder Bleeder Loves Crusher* (2024). This excerpt of *Lime Dill*

Halloween received the support of La Cité internationale de la bande dessinée et de l'image, in the form of an author residency at the Maison des Auteurs.

MARTA MONTEIRO's work has appeared on book covers, and in newspapers, children's books, and animation films. She has been a regular contributor to *The New York Times* and has also worked with *The New Yorker* and *Silvadesigners*. In 2014 she won a Gold Medal from the Society of Illustrators, and her animation film *Sopa Fria* was awarded Best Portuguese Short Film at the 2024 Monstra–Lisbon Animation Festival. She lives in the small town of Penafiel in Portugal, with her many cats.

AHMED NAJI is a bilingual writer, journalist, documentary filmmaker, and official criminal from Egypt. His novels are *Rogers* (2007), *Using Life* (2014), *And Tigers to My Room* (2020), *Happy Endings* (2023), and most recently a memoir, *Rotten Evidence: Reading and Writing in an Egyptian Prison* (McSweeney's, 2023), which was a finalist for the National Book Critics Circle Award. He is currently exiled in Las Vegas. More about his work can be found at ahmednaji.net.

MATT PANUSKA is an artist who works in illustration, zines, watercolor paintings, woodworking, and ink drawings. He is originally from the borderlands area of West Texas and lived in New York for many years. He now resides in Asheville, North Carolina. Folk imagery, golden age illustration, symbolist paintings, underground comix, surrealism, and many other sources inspire his artwork.

VALERIA PARRELLA is an Italian playwright and writer. She was born in Naples in 1974, and her first book, the short-story collection *Mosca più balena*, won Italy's Premio Campiello for best debut. Since then, she's gone on to write ten novels and three additional short-story collections, two of which were finalists for Italy's Premio Strega.

HANNAH PITTARD is the author of six books, most recently the novel *If You Love It, Let It Kill You*. She is the Guy M. Davenport Professor in English at the University of Kentucky and a winner of the Amanda Davis Highwire Fiction Award. She lives with her boyfriend and stepdaughter in Lexington, Kentucky. Much of her family lives nearby.

SONYA GRAY REDI was born in San Francisco and raised in Italy and California. She has a BA from UC San Diego and an MFA from Columbia University. Her work has appeared in *The Brooklyn Rail*, *The Rumpus*, and *Hobart*.

ENRICO ROTELLI is an Italian writer and journalist. His articles for *Corriere della Sera* on US literature are collected in *L'America è un esperimento*. He has translated *The Great Gatsby* by F. Scott Fitzgerald, and his most recent book is the autofiction *Nanda e io*. He's the recipient of the Premio Amerigo, the Premio Roberto Visintin, and the Premio Città di Como. He lives between San Francisco and Venice.

JOSEPHINE ROWE is the author of three story collections and two novels, including *A Loving, Faithful Animal* and *Here Until August*. Her fiction, poetry, and essays have been published widely, appearing in *Granta*, *Zoetrope: All-Story*, *The Believer*, *Freeman's*, *Neue Zürcher Zeitung*, and elsewhere. Her new novel, *Little World*, is forthcoming from Transit Books in the US. She currently lives in coastal Victoria, Australia.

JOANNA RUOCCO is the author of several books, including *Dan*, *Another Governess / The Least Blacksmith*, and *Field Glass*, coauthored with Joanna Howard. She also writes romance as Joanna Lowell. She teaches in the English Department at Wake Forest University.

LEANNE SHAPTON is an artist and writer. She is the author of *Important Artifacts and Personal Property from the Collection of Lenore Doolan and Harold Morris, Including Books, Street Fashion, and Jewelry*, and the children's book *Toys Talking*. Her memoir, *Swimming Studies*, won the 2012 National Book Critics Circle Award for autobiography. She is currently the art editor at *The New York Review of Books*.

JOSEPH EARL THOMAS is the author of the memoir *Sink*; the novel *God Bless You, Otis Spunkmeyer*, which won the Center for Fiction First Novel Prize; and the story collection *Leviathan Beach*. His writing has been published in places. Joseph teaches writing at Sarah Lawrence College, as well as courses in Black studies, poetics, video games, queer theory, and more at the Brooklyn Institute for Social Research.

DIANE WILLIAMS is the founder and editor of the literary annual *NOON*, the archive of which, as well as Williams's personal literary archive, was acquired in 2014 by the Lilly Library. She is the author of eleven books of fiction. Her most recent story collection is *I Hear You're Rich* (Soho Press).

CLOSE QUARTERS

Close Quarters members are a dedicated group of *McSweeney's Quarterly* subscribers who fervently believe that independent publishing is crucial for a culture of free, vibrant expression. Together, we're dedicated to telling the untold stories of our time, and providing readers with a sense of hope and adventure. McSweeney's publishes elegant books and periodicals that capture the complexity of the human experience, and our literary arts programs provide meaningful opportunities for readers, writers, and artists. Close Quarters members are crucial to making our work possible.

Join us. Donate via our online store, or, to learn more, please contact Amanda Uhle at amanda@mcsweeneys.net.

Our heartfelt thanks to these Close Quarters members. They are cherished friends whose support is crucial to the work we do.

Adam Blanchard	Jonathan Parker
Carli Cutchin	Gina & Dave Pell
Carol Davis	Jed Repko
Brian Dice	Sanchia Semere
Mark Fisher	Jessica Silverman
Brett Goldblatt	Alex Tievsky
Jonathan Huang	Caro Unger
Jordan Kurland	Johanne Wolfe
Chris Moultrie	Cameo Wood

AVAILABLE *from* McSWEENEY'S

ART AND COMICS

BOOKS FOR CHILDREN

PLAYS

HUMOR

COLLINS LIBRARY

ALL THIS AND MORE AT
STORE.MCSWEENEYS.NET

Founded in 1998, McSweeney's is an independent publisher based in San Francisco. McSweeney's exists to champion ambitious and inspired new writing, and to challenge conventional expectations about where it's found, how it looks, and who participates. We're here to discover things we love, help them find their most resplendent form, and place them into the hands of curious, engaged readers.

THERE ARE SEVERAL WAYS TO SUPPORT MCSWEENEY'S:

Support Us on Patreon
visit *www.patreon.com/mcsweeneysinternettendency*

Subscribe & Shop
visit *store.mcsweeneys.net*

Volunteer & Intern
email *bryce@thebeliever.net*

Sponsor Books & *Quarterlies*
email *amanda@mcsweeneys.net*

To learn more, please visit *www.mcsweeneys.net/donate*
or contact Executive Director Amanda Uhle at
amanda@mcsweeneys.net or 415.642.5609.

McSweeney's Literary Arts Fund is a nonprofit
organization as described by IRS 501(c)(3).
Your support is invaluable to us.